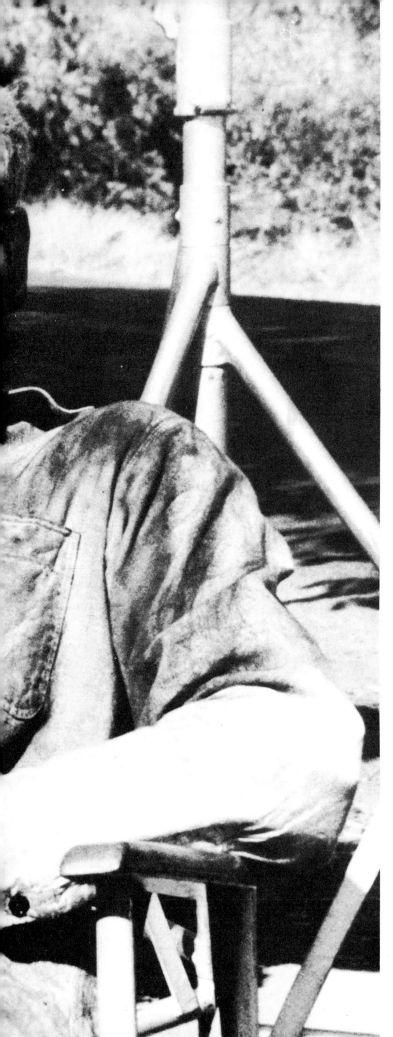

PAUL NEWMAN

J. C. LANDRY

McGRAW-HILL BOOK COMPANY

NEW YORK ST. LOUIS SAN FRANCISCO BOGOTÁ
GUATEMALA HAMBURG LISBON MADRID MEXICO
PANAMA PARIS SAN JUAN SÃO PAULO TOKYO

1 2 3 4 5 6 7 8 9 0 SEM SEM 8 7 6 5 4 3

First published in Great Britain in 1983 by Sidgwick and Jackson Limited

ISBN 0-07-036189-4

Library of Congress Cataloging in Publication Data

Landry, J.C.
  Paul Newman: an illustrated biography.
  Bibliography: p.
  Filmography: p.
  Includes index.
  1. Newman, Paul, 1925–   2. Moving-picture actors and actresses—United States—Biography.
I. Title.
PN2287.N44L36 1983   791.43′028′0924 [B]   83-9870
ISBN 0-07-036189-4

Book design by Rudolf Dixon

Previous pages: On the set of Cool Hand Luke, *1967*
Right: With Melvyn Douglas in Hud, *1962*

4

CONTENTS

PROLOGUE

'It's the juice that counts', that was how Steve McQueen put it before the black crab got him and clawed him down.

And then there was Wayne and 'A man's gotta do what a man's gotta do', and what does that mean at the end of the day except he has to be true to himself, to attempt to stay noble in a shabby world.

It was a band of the elect, a small group only, who proclaimed that faith, who lived it, and who survived. And many did not. There was Clift, burned up on pills and booze, Dean alienated beyond recall, Brando whacked out on himself and no longer part of it, and Flynn who never grew old but died ungracefully. . . And then there were the women, Rita and Lana and, most amongst them, Marilyn following the dark arrow to the edge and over.

There's a high price to pay up there, a price in spirit and a price in blood. It takes strong nerves to survive, hang on and hold your own. It's the juice that counts.

So what does it take to be a star? What does it take to cross that frontier, to make the quantum leap from well-paid actor to one who, suddenly, becomes heroic in stature, charismatic in radiance, mythic in renown? Or, in other words, to step from a million a picture to five times that amount plus a slab of the action? To become a giant in the industry and to call the shots . . . an explosive transition, happening on the instant, which can turn the head of any man and does of many.

How to survive then, to hang on to that basis which underpins the character of any man, which makes him what he is, his integrity?

So Newman is rare.

Now earning five million dollars plus per picture, he has not merely survived within a fickle and inconsequent industry, he has prevailed. And no one speaks ill of him, that is the truth which comes at you from the moment you start to learn about his life. He has acted shabbily to none.

Somebody Up There Likes Me, the tag and title of the picture which first launched him has followed him through life. At first sight he seems graced by luck as by a gift from God. Born of rich and loving parents, blessed by staggeringly good looks, intelligence and an athlete's skill, he never had to strive.

Already esteemed by audiences and within his profession, with *Butch Cassidy and The Sundance Kid* in 1972 he became international cinema's number one box office draw, the highest-paid actor in the world. He is an established film director with award-winning films to his credit. He has five children whom he loves and is loved by deeply. He enjoys a happy marriage with a gifted, intelligent friend which has endured for twenty-five years and remains rock-solid amongst the short-optioned liaisons and fragmented lifestyles of a surrounding landscape littered with human wreckage. Newman, you would say, is the man who has everything.

Yet – as with all golden coins which lie glittering in the sun – there is a reverse side. Beyond that candid gaze and the piercing blue eyes hides a shadowed being whose presence is uniquely hidden away.

The prosperous suburban background that spawned him was a gilded cage to the boy who grew up in it. Possessed by an inner restlessness, the anti-hero not yet created, he was a rebel looking for a cause. The roles in which he is most memorable, most convincing, most renowned, are paradoxically at odds with his rich conservative upbringing. From Hud to Harper, Rocky to Butch, again and again he has portrayed the loner, the underdog, the misfit and the psychopath: his *alter ego*, that darker self which lurks within him, whom he might have been had life gone differently.

And, along with that mirror self whose persona is oddly chilling stands another Newman who, by contrast, is wholly human.

Reticent, always in control, he has never imposed his troubles upon his public, yet he has known disaster as well as triumph. He, too, has passed a season in Hell and experienced those tragedies of death and loss and guilt and pain and inner crisis which are lived and shared by all of us.

A superstar, is the full sense of the word, Newman is a man as well.

At the 35th Annual Honorary Awards Banquet, 1973

1

THE BOY FROM THE RIGHT SIDE OF THE TRACKS

It was 26 January 1925. Cleveland, Ohio, lay under three feet of snow, whipped by a cruel wind off Lake Erie. The temperature was 14 degrees below freezing. For the inhabitants of the city it was a winter's day like any other.

For the young couple, Arthur and Teresa Newman, however, the date was memorable and particularly happy.

That morning Teresa had given birth to their second son, Paul, an unusually handsome baby of 8 pounds. His wide and alert eyes were the feature which all who saw him for the first time remarked upon. Unlike the clouded eyes of most new-born infants, his were an astonishing and piercing blue.

A comfortable and advantaged childhood awaited him, a stable home life and a good education. Later, it was expected, he would enter the family business, marry the right kind of girl, and take his rightful place within the community.

Prominent in their thriving and prosperous community, Newman's parents were second-generation Americans, his father, Arthur, of German-Jewish origin and his mother, Teresa, Hungarian-Catholic. It was an interesting mix and combined to make a good marriage, the contrasting backgrounds serving to complement and strengthen their union.

Teresa came from a highly distinguished Ohio family, mild-mannered and ladylike with a sensitivity that expressed itself in a strong moral concern for her fellow beings. Quite suddenly, she had converted to Christian Science and the children were raised within its rule. However, her new religion did not really 'take' on her sons who were more influenced by their father, a man with a powerful though conventional personality.

Newman Senior owned a flourishing sporting goods business in Cleveland; Paul and his brother, Arthur, grew up in a gracious eleven-roomed house, set in the exclusive and desirable suburb of Shaker Heights. A few miles outside the city, this was a zoned and landscaped ghetto of lavish private homes with spacious gardens. It was the preserve of the rich and successful, of those who held the most eminent positions in Cleveland. With privilege went respectability. It was not an environment to encourage the unusual or tolerate the eccentric. The Newmans did not flaunt their wealth; though they did not partake much in the snobbish round that composed social life in Shaker Heights, they were highly respected, well-liked and popular.

Although neither strict nor overly orthodox in the practice of his faith, Newman Senior taught the boys to live by its values. Despite the fact that money was abundant in the household, nothing was given them easily. Their father never spoiled his children, who learned early that rewards needed to be earned and gifts were an expression of love.

While all the other neighbourhood boys sported flashy baseball mitts (bought from the family store) at the ages of six or seven, it was not until he was ten that Paul received his first one. It was a training that served him well. In later life, surrounded on all sides by flagrant displays of wanton extravagance, he was never tempted to brag or show off.

Ostentation was to be avoided, yet Newman grew up secure in the certainty of wealth and with all the benefits of a close and loving family. He was sent to the best schools. His boyhood interests were encouraged and catered for. His father's brother, Joe, was a newspaperman, a poet and a song-writer; it was he who encouraged the young Newman to become a voracious reader.

Cleveland was a thriving city, but no centre of intellectual life. Paul was fortunate in his Uncle Joe, a man who believed a child's mind is not a vessel to be filled but a flame to be kindled. He was guided towards the great writers, and literature was brought alive for him in a manner lacking in the schools which he attended. In the trouble-free, idyllic but cloistered existence in which he was raised, these books opened a window on other worlds, other lives.

Theatre did not play a major role in the Shaker Heights community and Newman's identification with the cinema heroes of the time – Gable, Cooper, Cagney and Robinson – was minimal. He conceived no secret dreams of one day joining their ranks. If there was an early passion, it was for sport, although in this, too, his talents would develop only later, in his teens. With his good looks and genial personality he was popular and seemed content enough with all that life so far had given him. But throughout his childhood a creative propensity lay contained within the fabric of his family life. Apart from his Uncle Joe, his mother, Teresa, influenced her young son's tastes.

Teresa loved plays. They were her passion. She regularly attended the Hanna Theatre in Cleveland, and this shy and sensitive woman came to life whenever she spoke of the theatre. Each time she came home after these plays she would describe in detail all she had seen to her younger son.

Thus encouraged by his mother, Newman took part in many school productions as a child, at the age of seven playing a clown in *Robin Hood* and singing a song written by his Uncle Joe. A great success, he enjoyed his family's pride in the performance.

Left: Boy from the right side of the tracks

Page 11: New boy in Hollywood

At ten he acted for the first time before a proper audience. Performing at the Cleveland Playhouse in *St George and the Dragon*, he played St George himself. The dragon was a placid old bulldog, and the climax of the play involved the triumph of St George over this ferocious beast. To achieve a semblance of authentic fury salt was poured on to the tail of the unfortunate creature and results were satisfactory, though the bulldog-dragon himself was none too pleased.

Newman recalls with surprise how totally at ease he felt at this exposure to the public. Yet no one took these clues seriously at the time, for such activity was regarded only as a childish pastime.

The picture seems too perfect. A certain blandness pervades the golden childhood of this regular, all-American suburban kid. Where was the edge, the shadow of that special difference which distinguishes some individuals from others, causing them to stir from out of the crowd and to step forward into the spotlight of fame and public recognition?

There were no dark moods in this sunny child, no visible dissatisfaction, yet, even then, some outsiders did detect a difference, a fatalistic streak, a reckless assurance. During his schooldays a young girl in the class below adored him from afar. Though he was no more than fourteen or fifteen at the time, she thought of him as a 'real' man and today recalls exactly her first impression of him: 'He was strikingly attractive . . . there was something dangerous about him, you felt he was not really tamed, that just beneath the surface there was a streak of violence. . . '

Nothing in Newman's outward behaviour or words demonstrated this unnerving sense of danger and unpredictability. Only much later would rebellion come.

He showed no striking talents at school, nor did he experience any abysmal failures. Just above average, he was one of those students of whom it was said, 'he shows promise'. He could always notch up a passing grade without apparent effort. He accomplished everything without effort; all who knew him in those days remember that enviable facility.

His activities outside of school were the classic pastimes of boyhood – fishing, playing baseball, running wild with other boys, tobogganing and skating during the long winters, when snow lay deep across the country, climbing trees, and occasionally getting into scrapes. He was also something of a neighbourhood clown, and in this fashion some of his buried talents found an outlet. He often 'acted around', made faces with appalling accuracy of expression, yodelled and sang at untoward moments, and such antics sometimes led him into mischief.

His relationship with his brother Arthur, one year older, showed little sibling rivalry. Arthur was an engaging, easy-going boy who was never overbearing but merely affectionate and protective. Later, after Paul's huge successes, they stayed close, with Arthur taking a working interest in the business affairs of his more creative younger brother.

Paul was an endearing and interesting child, although the restraints of the society he grew up in did not enable him to go beyond an acceptable and normal interpretation of individuality. As if by instinct, he knew just how far he could push this in terms of self-assertion. But, although he was always something of a fighter, he never strayed too far from the closely-defined standards of his fellows.

Perhaps his unique qualities would have found earlier expression had it not been for one factor – from the moment he first entered the world Newman was beautiful to look upon. It was not a matter of being merely attractive. So handsome he was, so fine and noble of feature – whilst those eyes grew ever more startling in their colour, with an unsettling candour in their gaze – that his looks were considered 'wasted on a boy'. All who saw him were struck by his appearance.

For those born with such singular advantage, the usual trials and tribulations of acceptance by one's peers, the sheer competitive efforts required through being young and making one's mark, are strangely eased. There was no need to *try* for recognition. Automatically, it was granted him. People cannot help but respond to physical beauty and good looks are irresistibly attractive when combined with amiability and good nature.

But all this good fortune can present its own disadvantages. When young, when things are too easy, an individual can avoid the tempering which comes with adversity. For Newman there was no incentive to excel, only the basic requirement to get by.

There was, however, one thing that saved him from his beauty; he was without vanity. While he responded to those who reacted to his looks, he himself was not overly aware of them. He responded to these people simply because he was interested in them, a quality he retains today, and an essential characteristic of the actor. This lack of self-consciousness of his looks was as attractive as the looks themselves. It implied a stability, a sureness of self and a confidence born of innate good sense.

This popular, beautiful child, then, not too clever to daunt nor dull enough to dismiss, was perfectly suited to the expectations of Shaker Heights. Surely his fate was sealed? His grades would always be passable, he would graduate without difficulty, take over the family business, marry a suitable local girl and become the pillar of American society that his father had been before him. As a candidate he was perfect, the ideal.

But fate had other plans. Within him lay a time bomb, ticking towards its moment. One day it would explode and blow apart the life that everyone expected. No one guessed at that bomb's existence, least of all himself. But the future of young Paul Newman lay far beyond the staple dreams and homely aspirations of Shaker Heights.

Adolescence came and with it the usual preoccupations of that period – sport, awareness of girls, and commitment to new ideas and interests. At Shaker Heights High School he became known for his skill in debate. Articulate, he grabbed the attention of his audience with his potent delivery – another of the clues to his latent talent. He had been encouraged in this ability to dissect ideas by the advantage of living within a communicative family. 'Talking things through' with his father or literary-minded uncle was a normal part of daily life in the household.

It was during these years that his love of sport began to manifest itself. At first just scraping into his class football team, his skills gradually developed to the point where he considered it as a career. A real interest in drama became evident, although Newman still had no thoughts of becoming an actor. While he was at Shaker Heights he participated in many plays, both as player and as stage-manager.

Newman has always been self-effacing about his achievements and seems almost to take pleasure in insisting upon his mediocrity at school and college. The observations of those who knew him at the time belie the image of such dullness and make more sense of the man he would become. William Walton, his English coach, recalls: 'He was extremely intelligent and, unusual for a high school boy, was interested in serious drama.'

The seeds for the future had already been sown, though for many years yet they would lie dormant, thwarted in an indifferent, even hostile environment, which did not rate these qualities in its young highly. More important was practical success, being part of a team, preparing for the competitive and corporate world of adulthood. Young Newman, like other sons of Shaker Heights, worked through his vacations. It was part of the culture he had been born into, where the men with the best skill in negotiating, bargaining, buying, and selling, achieved the most respected positions and were most admired. Young Newman took a job at Danny Budin's Corned Beef Palace, a local sandwich bar.

It was not until he was sixteen that the previously gregarious boy began to disappear alone for hours, tramping through the streets of Cleveland with his dog, Cleo. The habit was noted, but what went on inside the young man's head remains a mystery to all but himself. The quality of elusiveness, a characteristic of many successful and famous people, is a tantalizing trait that excites curiosity in all who encounter it. Newman, even then, possessed this quality. People recognized a separateness, a confidence from within that sustained and guided him unaided by friends and family. He was truly independent. A stubbornness and polite defiance began to reveal itself in small ways. The submerged complexities of his personality were brewing in a stew of adolescent upheaval. Not yet fully identified or understood, they agitated and disturbed him in the classic turbulence of the teenage years. Yet he contained and controlled this restlessness, and his loyalties still lay within the conventional expectations of his family and the society in which he lived.

In 1943, Newman left Shaker Heights High and for a while 'dropped out', aimless, unmotivated and restless. He drifted from job to job, embracing anything that caught his imagination, only to move on again, guided by accident or by fate. His most successful venture at this time was as a door-to-door salesman.

'To see whether I could sell myself to people', he decided to take a job selling encyclopaedias. It was akin to learning how to swim by throwing himself into the deep end, selling in its crudest, most demanding, even embarrassing, form. Newman was undaunted. Unconscious of the fact that he was acting, he charmed these strangers at their doors, skilfully adapting to the different personalities, genders and types that confronted him. Instinctively, he found he was able to act out the responses appropriate to the person. Not only did he succeed in 'selling himself': on completing his final sale he pocketed a profit of $500.

And then, on the rare occasions when he talks of that period, Paul lets slip another hint of the as-yet unacknowledged lure of the profession he would embrace. With the $500 profit he embarked on his next scheme. He became an entrepreneur, and mounted a theatrical show. It was a foolhardy venture – the show was amateurish, unco-

ordinated and doomed to failure. When it flopped the $500 disappeared with it. However, it was a brave enterprise in one so young, and although Newman regarded it as a business investment, there can be no doubt that his choice had been influenced by his ever-growing interest in drama.

He then worked at his father's store for a while, this time a victim of his good-natured parent's ethical code. He was expected to show up half an hour earlier than other staff and to leave half an hour later at night. He was also paid less than his workmates. To his father, nepotism was deplorable, and favouritism unworthy and damaging for everyone concerned.

Newman laboured under dutiful obligation, with a real fear of disappointing his elders. Yet, although anxious to please, he simply did not enjoy being in business. Though he concealed the fact, he hated it. At the same time he had no alternative to offer for his future and, reluctantly, agreed to study economics and business training. He entered Ohio University, in Athens, Ohio. From the beginning, Newman's heart was not in his studies, but before discontent had time to develop into something worse, his problems were temporarily solved by events outside his control.

At 7.55 a.m. on 7 December 1941, when Newman was nearly seventeen years old, the Japanese airforce, commanded by Vice-Admiral Chuichi Nagumo, attacked Pearl Harbour. The battleship *Arizona* and seventeen naval ships were sunk or severely damaged and 170 U.S. aeroplanes were destroyed. Some 2,897 servicemen perished and the lives of Newman and his fellow citizens were brutally re-arranged.

He had been at Ohio University for only one term when the attack took place. Like thousands of other young men he left to enlist in the Navy. Volunteering to become a pilot, he was selected for the Naval Air Corps V.12 education programme and his group was sent to Yale University for a specialized course.

This venerable establishment, with its stimulating ethos of intellectual adventure, was an immediate inspiration. Yale, and all that it represented, struck a nerve. It was love at first sight. For the first time he found a platform from which to examine his ideas, and his eyes opened to a world wider and more diverse than his provincial background had led him to believe existed.

Sadly, this happy and inspiring episode in his life ended after four months. A routine check-up revealed a flaw in the now-famous blue eyes – he was colour blind. The disappointed would-be flyer was dropped from the programme.

Reluctantly, he left the cloistered campus which had revealed so much to him, determined one day to return. He served then as a radio man on torpedo planes in the Pacific, based on Okinawa, Guam and Hawaii. He had entered the war with his mind in turmoil. He knew now what he wished to do next with his life – return to Yale to study. He also knew that he might die. For the first time he confronted fear.

Newman's war held one chilling experience that remains forever imprinted on his mind. After a series of flying missions, the pilot in charge of his squadron one day developed an ear infection and, that morning, the squadron was stood down. Early that same afternoon, when the replacement squadron sat fully kitted up within the Ready Room, a Japanese Kamikazi plane, charged with high explosives,

which had been stalking the aircraft carrier, plummeted from the cloud layer. The speed and force of its dive ripped a hole clear through the deck and into the Ready Room where it exploded, killing everyone within.

It was Newman's first experience of death, and it had come very close to him. He was awed by the experience. His life had been saved by an accident, by luck.

He spent two years in the Navy and apart from this incident Newman recalls an otherwise uneventful war: 'Those years were spent drinking and reading everything that came into my hands. When I was at Hawaii, Guam and Saipan I was reading ten or fifteen books per week. Just at the moment when I thought I'd see some action the Atomic Bomb was dropped and the war was over.'

He was demobilized in April 1946 and returned to his studies on the G.I. Bill. He enrolled in Kenyon College, Ohio, and resumed his courses in banking and economics. But he had grown up during those two years and become more decisive. He had no interest in finance and finally accepted the fact that a career in business was out of the question. The decision lifted a weight from him. He switched to literature and drama and, liberated from 'doing the right thing', began at last really to enjoy life. He developed a prowess for beer drinking and took his pick from a campus full of eager adoring girls. Females went belly up before him but were soon made painfully aware of his elusiveness. He loved them and left them, preferring to play the field without commitment. Despite envy of this success, Newman was well-liked and popular with his male associates.

It was now that his proficiency in sport developed to the point where he not only became something of a football hero but he actually considered turning professional. Playing in his college team, it was ironically an incident that occurred as a result of football that was responsible for changing the course of his life.

He and some other members of the team were drinking in a bar one night when they became involved in a brawl with some local boys. The incident grew sufficiently ugly for someone to telephone the police. Six college boys were arrested, including Newman. They were put into cells and, when the case was heard, two were expelled from Kenyon and the remaining four – one of them Newman – put on probation and thrown out of the team.

It was the first time he had got into any kind of serious trouble – and to the law-abiding citizens of Shaker Heights this was trouble, mortifying and public. Newman's parents were upset but knew their son had been more than adequately punished. To be dropped from the team was a serious setback, the death blow to his greatest passion. It hurt him deeply and he experienced considerable shame over the whole affair.

Fortunately he was resilient by nature. Shortly after this episode, the College drama department announced that they were auditioning for a forthcoming play. Newman recalls what happened next. 'I was damned if I was going to let my football disgrace interfere with my extra-curricular activities . . . I went along to read for the lead part and got it. I played Hildy Johnson in *The Front Page*, a corker of a play

The straight actor, 1958

which still has a lot of mileage in it, and we got a big reception. I took several bows and had my first heady taste of acting.'

At once all the enthusiasm he had previously devoted to sport was now poured into drama. He appeared in a series of college productions and dedicated himself to absorbing everything which pertained to theatre. While he had no notion yet of becoming a professional actor, the die had been cast.

Meanwhile, the uncompleted business studies proved to have their use. With time on his hands he decided to go in for a modest yet shrewd commercial venture: 'I found a little bin of a shop for rent in the high street and converted it into a laundry. As a special service I offered my customers – all college kids – free beer on the side. I figured this would make the laundry chores more pleasant all round as well as knock the opposition laundries out of business . . . I soon became a monopoly. With low rental and profits after investing in the beer, I was taking at least $60 a week for myself.'

Clearly, if fate had not already marked out an alternative future, Newman could have become an astute businessman, despite his antagonism towards the trade. His description of this smart little operation demonstrates something of his father's quality of hard-headed acumen combined with humanity. It is interesting to note that in later life this inborn shrewdness re-emerged as Newman moved into film production and set up his own corporations.

All of that was yet to come . . . but now the seed had become a budding plant. All that was needed was the right time and the right place, the suitable climate for the bud to flower. The road ahead was still unclear but it led in the right direction. Newman was on his way.

Newman with his brother Arthur

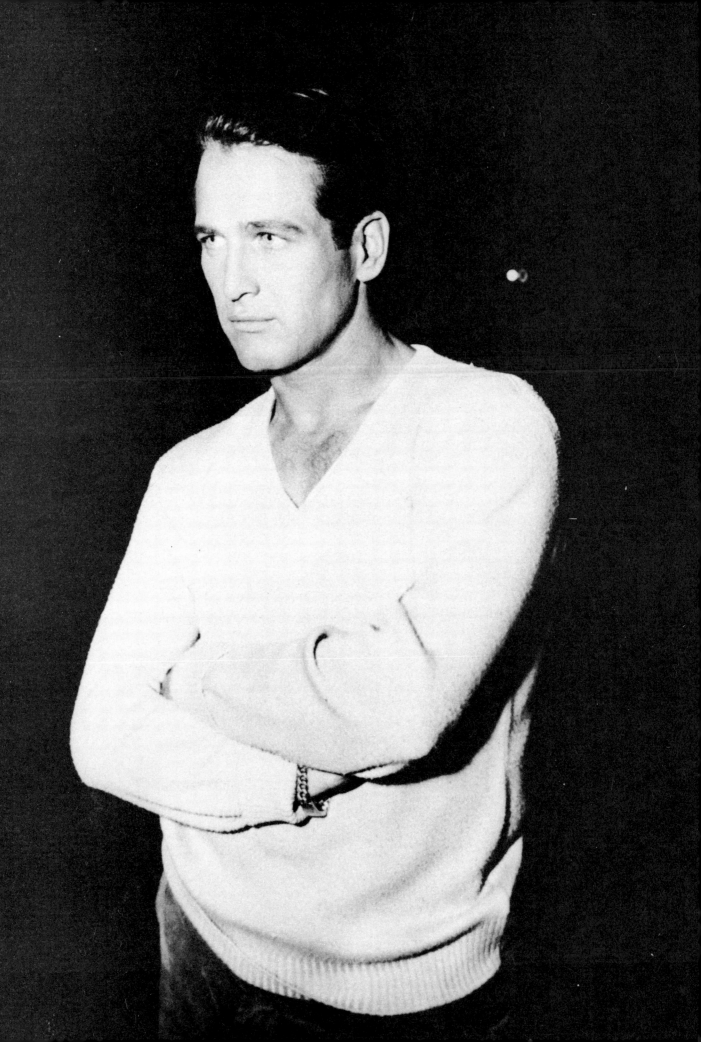

58

2
A REGULAR GUY WITH IRREGULAR NOTIONS

Paul Newman graduated from Kenyon College on 3 June 1949 with a Bachelor of Science degree. The ceremony took place at 2 o'clock and by 4 that same afternoon he was on a train to Williams Bay, Wisconsin. Together with the diploma in his pocket was a contract to join an acting tour in summer stock.

Still with no vision of his future, as if by instinct he had chosen the appropriate path. Newman at the time was unaware of it. On leaving college he recalls: 'I didn't know what to do. So I drifted into summer stock.' The decision to act was not accompanied by any driving urge to make a name for himself. 'When I decided to become an actor I wasn't looking for my identity, I was simply running away from the family business. To be an actor was a happy alternative to a style of life which meant nothing to me.'

Even after he had arrived at Williams Bay and found great pleasure in his work, he was still inclined towards a professorship. Interpreting roles and appearing on stage were interesting, even exciting, activities but not realistic goals. His main aim in life was to avoid selling sports equipment. But with hindsight Newman is able to recognize that, unconsciously, he felt the pull towards theatre. 'Actually,' he says, 'when people start to do something, they *are* heading towards a goal.'

At Williams Bay Newman had his first experience of non-college acting. The atmosphere in the company was informal, pleasant and easy. Questioning 'straight society' – of which his own background was a definitive example – formed a frequent subject of group discussion. Heated arguments on moral issues, however emotionally charged, were regarded as a natural and human function of everyday life. Newman was stimulated by the openness and fervour displayed by his more worldly colleagues. An awareness that had first revealed itself during the short but happy months at Yale now became part of his conscious thinking. He did not like the double standards he recognized in society. He was maturing, developing an edge, growing less bland, becoming less and less the 'regular guy'.

With the company at Williams Bay he learned the basics of his craft, not only through acting but in stage management

and involvement in the entire process of production from concept to box office. Most important of all, he started to recognize where his heart lay and, although he would wait several years for the rewards of success, that he wanted to be involved in this world. It was more than merely a diversion.

In the autumn of that same year Newman moved on to join another company, The Woodstock Players in Illinois, with whom he appeared in several productions, among them *Suspect, Cyrano de Bergerac, The Candlestick Maker, Dark of the Moon*, and *The Glass Menagerie*.

During this carefree period Newman fell in love for the first time. Another of his Woodstock productions was Norman Krasner's *John and Mary*, in which he took the part of a soldier. The other main part was played by a young brown-eyed, blonde actress named Jackie Witte. Jackie was a highly intelligent, funny and articulate young woman who returned Newman's feelings towards her with an ardour that matched his own. The first person in his life to understand something of his inner complexity and discontent and to recognize his need to act, she was quite unlike the campus sweethearts and suitable young ladies with whom he had associated before. Jackie was strong in her views, original in her thinking, sensitive and talented. At the time she was exactly what he needed.

After a lightning courtship they slipped away to get married in the spring of 1949. At the end of summer they rejoined the company in Illinois. During that winter Newman appeared in sixteen plays, among which were productions of *Our Town, Meet Me in St Louis, Mr Roberts* and *Born Yesterday*. In the spring of 1950 he took a break from theatre and worked as a labourer on a farm near Woodstock. But he was happy with his life, cheerfully anticipating the birth of his first child – for Jackie was now pregnant – while his ideas on his career were taking shape. It seemed that the course of his life was now set in the right direction.

A Regular Guy. On the set of Paris Blues, *1961*

Then suddenly, during that same year, his father fell seriously ill. The sense of guilt and duty of earlier days returned. There was no question but that he must return to Shaker Heights to support his mother and help run the family business. Newman and his wife, with their tiny baby Scott, packed their bags and moved to Cleveland into a house close to the family home. The carefree days were over, although he was able to support his little family more than adequately. Jackie could hardly bear to think of her non-conformist, dreamy young husband trapped within this restricted setting. She, more than anyone, suspected another destiny. The idea that the qualities and unique talent she had come to recognize should be wasted was intolerable. In those days she was his finest supporter. Yet, dutifully, she did not add to the burden of his problems by forcing the issue. She followed him back to Shaker Heights.

Newman had already demonstrated that he possessed sound business sense, despite the fact that it gave him little satisfaction. With a faint heart, inspired by zero enthusiasm, he worked hard and impressed his family and workmates by his achievements.

'I was very successful at being something I was not,' he says of that period, 'and that's the worst thing that can happen to a person. If you try to be something you aren't and fail – then you have a stronger motivation to change . . . but, when you succeed at being something you're not, it's a lot harder to break away.'

It was ironic that he was successful at something he hated. His months at work in the family business were the unhappiest and most depressing he experienced in his young life. 'I just couldn't find any romance in it,' he says in explanation of his aversion to business.

After several months of this existence the problem was resolved in the saddest possible way. In 1950 his father, Arthur, died. After a grim period of mourning a different perspective on life's obligations revealed itself to the dutiful son. The death of a father often brings with it a new sense of identity, a determination to continue as head of the family on one's own terms.

Adding strength to this new sense of self, in the same year of his father's death, Newman himself had become a father. Life had to go on and the baby's existence helped to fill the void.

Newman stayed on in Cleveland while the family business was sold. It was the end of an era. Meanwhile, he spent a short spell working at a golf club. His duties consisted of picking up the dirty balls and washing them so that they could be used again. It was not an inspiring occupation. During the same period he acted on a local radio station, for the advertising agency, McCann Erikson, and for a telephone and telegram company in Ohio.

But by the autumn of 1951 he could tolerate this existence no longer. At last free from guilt, sadder but wiser, he closed up the house, leaving Shaker Heights behind him to move on to the next and most critical phase of his life.

Newman was twenty-six years old when he finally made the break and, with his wife and small son, quit Shaker Heights forever.

With his modest savings from working in the family business he now returned to Yale and enrolled in the Drama School. His intention was to study to become a professor of English and he visualized himself teaching at his old college, Kenyon.

Newman, Jackie and their baby took a top-floor flat in a house in New Haven. Money was short and the rambling old building housed three other families in similar circumstances to themselves. But the young couple were happy. Newman had at last found himself in an environment that complemented his needs and inclination. Settling down quickly in his new neighbourhood, he found life in New Haven peaceful and pleasant. It was here that his enduring affection for New England was born. He enjoyed the civilized, urbane attitudes he met there and was beguiled by the beauty of the surrounding country.

Although the courses Newman had chosen specialized in the *mechanics* of drama production and much of his practical studies were concentrated on directing, he still performed on stage. He appeared in six one-act plays and at least four full-length projects. Even in these early performances at Yale his charismatic talent was evident to others.

Frank McMullan, associate professor of Production at Yale, recalls one prophetic occasion: 'The theatre agents, Liebling and Wood, came to New Haven to see the play [about the life of Beethoven with Newman cast as the composer's nephew] but were more impressed by Paul Newman as a potential actor than in the stage-worthiness of the play. The production was presented in the spring and through it Paul [later] landed his first job in theatre in William Inge's very successful play *Picnic*. Of course this meant that he left the Drama School . . .'

Although no one realized it at the time, that night was the beginning of it all. By now, quite apart from his inborn, natural talent, Newman had acquired years of experience which had added to his stature as an actor. But this performance was his definitive breakthrough.

Yet, even now, he held back. Pressure to pursue acting had come from others. Already some of his tutors at Yale had hinted that Broadway was where his future lay. Newman remained unconvinced. He knew that career would be a rat race, and he envisaged a calmer, more secure existence for his family. Influenced by the values instilled in his childhood, he regarded teaching as a more sensible and serious occupation.

But the heat was on. As his admirers continually extolled his skills, Newman came to accept that acting was in his blood.

The lure was irresistible. Still, the decision to abandon his studies was hard to make. Jackie encouraged her husband to follow his instincts. Theatre in New York was in a flux of experiment and innovation. The timing was ideal for an actor of Newman's youth and calibre. It would mean uprooting the family once more, of course, but that was the least of Jackie's concerns. His career came first. Two years later, after Yale, might be too late. The new era in New York presented a golden opportunity. Plays were being imported from Europe and alternative theatres were springing up everywhere. The climate was perfect.

The final decision was reached one night when Jackie asked Newman what was stopping him. He had no real answer.

And so, once more, the family packed their bags and all their worldly goods in the beat-up car and moved on.

At the world premiere of A Little Romance, *1979*

He had decided to give himself just one year to find out if he could survive in the cut-throat world of New York theatre. He would do everything possible to make it work, follow up every contact, take any offer however lowly.

Meanwhile, he had one year. If at the end of this time he had allotted himself he failed to meet his target, he would return to Yale to follow his original plan.

For the moment, however, cash was running out and he needed any kind of work to pay for somewhere to live. Before he could even consider enrolling at the Actors' Studio, a move he regarded as essential, yet more money would be necessary for classes.

It was the summer of 1952. For a few days the Newmans stayed in a modest hotel before finding an apartment in a peaceful backwater on Long Island, close to the home of an aunt of Jackie's. It was a perfect compromise, far enough from New York to provide peace, yet close enough to keep in touch with theatrical action. Another consideration was the healthier environment of Long Island for growing children, with the Atlantic only minutes from the apartment. Then there was Jackie's aunt who would babysit, so they could get out alone together from time to time. For now Jackie was expecting their second child. She had decided against a career of her own. One actor in the family was enough. She felt no resentment. She had always wanted a family and enjoyed the role of motherhood.

It was a long, hot summer. Newman would leave home each morning at 8 a.m., dressed in his only decent suit. Stepping off the ferry at Manhattan he would tramp the streets for hours on a tour of all the agents, stopping for a coffee to read the small ads in the trade papers. This became a daily ritual.

In spite of the cheap apartment there were hefty financial commitments and his need for work was drastic. It soon became apparent that the mechanics of their lives could not be managed without a car, but running costs were high. Large telephone bills were an occupational hazard. Appearances, of a sort, had to be kept up within the competitive world of New York. Being where the action was cost money, too. Staying in touch with others in the business meant obligatory drinks and meals. For a while it was a struggle to survive.

He was lucky. Within a month he had landed his first job, a brief appearance in a television drama, *The March of Time*, in which he played an old man – at a fee of $65. He was tenacious in his hunt for parts and his efforts reaped rewards. During the next three months he appeared in several small television roles and finally succeeded in getting a regular spot in a soap opera, *The Aldwych Family*. These jobs were hardly prestigious and television did not pay well in those days. However, his contacts and reputation grew and with them his ambitions.

The small apartment on Long Island no longer seemed satisfactory. Newman wanted to be in the heart of it all, yet Jackie had by now given birth to their second child, Susan, and the family remained on the Island. But it was New York that was really home. Newman had come to love the city as it was then. He recalls his impressions with enthusiasm: 'When I first went to New York it was a simple joy just to walk along Broadway and feel that, with luck, you might get into the theatrical scene with a really worthwhile part. Marvellous new plays by people like Rod Stirling and Paddy Chayefsky were being performed live on television. Arthur

Miller and Tennessee Williams were bringing fresh concepts into drama. It was the kind of action I imagined to have taken place in Elizabethan London. I wanted a piece of that action and getting into television was the first step.'

At last Newman had discovered the key to himself. 'I spent nearly the first thirty years of my life looking for a way to explode,' he says, 'For me, apparently, acting is that way.'

Soon he had established himself on the television networks and work became regular. His face grew familiar to audiences. He landed important parts as time went by, amongst them a starring role in the musical adaptation of Thornton Wilder's *Our Town* with co-stars Frank Sinatra and Eva Marie Saint. It was 1953.

It was during this time that his next big breakthrough came, though it had been written in the stars since his Yale performance as Beethoven's nephew. The agents, Liebling and Wood, who had seen and been so impressed by that portrayal, arranged for him to meet the playwright William Inge, who was casting for the Broadway production of his play *Picnic*. The young actor was called for an audition. Newman got the part, that of an inexperienced college boy who loses his girl to a more worldly classmate.

The play, directed by Joshua Logan, was a huge success and Newman's performance was singled out for critical acclaim. Richard Watts of the *New York Post* reported: 'Paul Newman has done an excellent job.' Joe Chapman of the *New York Daily News* declared: 'The rich boy was very well played by Paul Newman.' Robert Coleman of the *New York Daily Mirror* wrote: 'Paul Newman was excellent.' Brooks Atkinson in the prestigious *New York Times* was moved to say, ' . . . Paul Newman knows how to express the sensitive aspect of the character . . . As a college lad infatuated with pretty faces . . . he brings to life all the cross currents of Mr Inge's sensitive writing.' The play launched Newman's professional career on stage.

Picnic ran for fourteen months and, financially secure, he was now able to seek acceptance at the Actors' Studio, his motive for coming to New York. Entry requirements were tough but with a reputable success under his belt he felt ready to take his chances.

Once more, good luck worked for him; a young actress also auditioning needed a man to play opposite her and asked Newman. He agreed, supported her scene and helped to make it work.

Before an actor could be considered for acceptance at the Studio he was obliged to do two auditions, the first in front of an audience. If he passed this test he moved on to the second audition, this time before such critical notables as Elia Kazan and Cheryl Crawford.

However, somehow wires got crossed and only a few days after the actress's audition Newman received notice that he had been accepted to the Actors' Studio. Technically, he had not even auditioned but his supporting role had ensured him a place.

This period with the Actors' Studio was the greatest influence not only in his career but also his own life. The very nature of the so-called Method – the belief that you must become the part you play – enabled Newman to understand more about himself. He began to analyse his feelings about his background together with his parents' attitudes and expectations. He still felt enormous guilt at moving away so completely from his family and was uncomfortable with this speedy escape so soon after his father's death. At times he

felt it would have been more suitable if he had remained at Yale to become a teacher.

He started to air his feelings in the easy communion of the Actors' Studio and began a number of lifelong friendships with fellow students Geraldine Page, Julie Harris, Eli Wallach and Rod Steiger. Later, even after he had fully established himself, he would return to the Studio a couple of times a week whenever he was in New York, to rediscover his roots and hone his craft.

He made another friend during his New York period. Just prior to landing the part in *Picnic* he had met a young actress named Joanne Woodward. The meeting was uneventful and brief. Her first impression was that he was just another conservative college boy, while he considered her merely another of the countless actresses in a city filled with good-looking and ambitious ladies.

Then, quite by coincidence, Miss Woodward was cast as understudy to Janice Rule and Kim Stanley in *Picnic*. The two recalled their first meeting and their initial misconceptions were corrected. Their friendship blossomed during the run of the play, growing more affectionate as time went by. They got on extremely well together but submerged their feelings towards each other. Newman was a married man. Occasionally they would share a coffee and enjoy the bond of a common interest in their careers. But when Newman returned to his home and family in Long Island, Joanne led her own life. Neither had any premonition that one day they would live together.

Meanwhile, Newman was noticed by the moguls of Hollywood, always on the lookout for a new face. His was already a familiar countenance to the citizens of New York. In the streets people recognized him, coming up to say what they had seen him in.

Now Hollywood offered screen tests and the good life. At first he resisted. The expedience and commercialism of motion pictures was unattractive. It was not, he was sure, the best outlet for his talent. He did not like the idea of being bought.

Most of his fellow students at the Actors' Studio spoke of Hollywood with contempt. The 'star system' still existed, anathema to any serious actor. Newman was by now dedicated to his art, sure of good work, making fair money and happy in what he did. He was the father of two young children. He was contented with his life, his family was settled. To place all this at risk for the dubious advantages of a Hollywood career seemed too high a price.

And yet . . . For all his misgivings about Hollywood, he was aware that in an age of rapidly expanding communications, films were an essential element of an actor's experience. In New York, for all their professed contempt, most of the best actors already worked on pictures. For all their talk of hack directors and mediocrity, the fact remained that they were making movies.

Newman was now in his thirtieth year, an age for taking stock. He found himself unable to ignore the call. Warner Brothers had offered him a seven-year contract.

Shortly after *Picnic* closed, Newman finally decided to go west. Leaving Jackie and the children at home in Long Island, he packed his bags and, not without misgivings, headed for Los Angeles, the city of dreams.

At the opening of Waltz of the Toreador, *1973*

3
SOMEBODY UP THERE LIKES ME

The dream turned sour as soon as Newman arrived in Hollywood. He checked into a motel close to Warners and the moment he set foot in the studios his worst fears about 'the system' were confirmed. As he performed in the screen test that supposedly would make or break him, several businessmen watched, muttering among themselves as though he did not exist. When the test was completed it was clear that he had not much impressed them and he was despatched to Studio Hairdressing without ceremony. There they dyed his hair. It was not Newman's acting that had bothered them. In those days uniformity was all-important, both physically and creatively; if you could half-way act your way through a scene that was sufficient to satisfy the Hollywood moguls of the 1950s. Capped teeth and nose jobs were arbitrary commands dispensed from the executive Viewing Room.

Although they were on their last legs, the working attitudes and methods of the good old days still existed in Hollywood when Newman first arrived. Films were vehicles for stars, those who had already proved themselves at the box office. The talent of the actors and their suitability for the parts they were given were of secondary importance. Hollywood was in the business of profit; innovative ideas and original, unusual film projects were regarded as suspect and unnecessary risks. Business was conducted at lavish, drunken parties and the casting couch was still an executive instrument.

Publicity departments wielded enormous power and an actor's or actress's success with the general public, together with his or her reputation within the business, obliged him or her to conform to the image chosen to ensure popularity. The image was all that mattered.

Gossip columnists such as Hedda Hopper, Louella Parsons, Sheilah Graham and Radie Harris, wielded as great an influence as the studio heads themselves. More than 600 newspapers ran Parsons' column alone. Readership was phenomenal and there were also hundreds of lesser columnists to contend with. They formed a pernicious network that nothing escaped. They could release a story to the world which could make or break an individual.

Inspiring fear and loathing while feeding lavishly and successfully off this power, many became flamboyant celebrities in their own right – 'stars' themselves, the first to receive the most important invitations, the first to be honoured with the latest news and secrets. In order not to fail, never mind how talented, an actor or actress had to stick rigidly by the rules.

It was hard enough for those performers who had dedicated themselves single-mindedly to the pursuit of fame and recognition, much more for the man or woman who was a serious artiste. The system took its toll. To Newman it was sheer hell. Right from the start he saw beyond the superficial accoutrements of success as defined in Hollywood. Behind the façade of palatial homes with swimming pools, glossy parties and all the glamour, he saw how desperate and meaningless were the lives of most so-called stars. Drunks, pill freaks and lost identities were the norm. A man or woman was easily destroyed in such an atmosphere and Hollywood was faithless and cruel to its casualities. There was always someone to replace you. Booze and drugs numbed the senses and soothed the tensions. More analysts practised here than anywhere in the world.

There were exceptions, of course. Characters who would have survived anywhere, whose sense of self and worth was so established that nothing could crack their egos. Men like Humphrey Bogart, Kirk Douglas, Jack Lemmon and John Huston remained always true to themselves. Fortunately for Newman, with his innate good sense, there was never any possibility that he could be blinded and seduced by Hollywood.

Soon after he arrived he was cast by Warners in one of the least distinguished motion pictures of the 1950s. At the time a long-term contract with a major studio was the rule. There were almost no independent producers and an actor had to follow his studio's dictates. In Newman's case this first spectacle, but for his famous luck, could have been both the beginning and the end of his career in films.

The dreadful production was called *The Silver Chalice*. Newman's role was that of a Greek slave named Basil. The script was painful, containing such lines as: 'Oh, Helina, is it really you? What joy!' Newman had been chosen for his blue eyes and good physique and a passing resemblance to the successful rebel actor, Marlon Brando, rather than for any acting skill.

Such was his embarrassment at appearing in the film, Newman quickly gained a reputation in Hollywood as reticent and difficult. Humiliated and angry, he recalls his unhappiness at the time: 'So this was *it*. At the end of each day's filming I would go back to my motel feeling absolutely lousy. For months they came knocking at your door. You had reached the point where you were beginning to feel that empty space in your heart . . . wondering how long they'll keep knocking. I *had* to go to Hollywood. I *had* to sign a contract with one of the big companies, or get lost in the

At a rehearsal for the Inaugural Gala at the Kennedy Center, 1977

shuffle. What I hadn't anticipated was the absolute disaster of being cast in a lousy film.'

Years later, the film was scheduled for an entire week's run on L.A. television. The Newmans took out a newspaper advertisement bordered by a black memorial wreath. It read: 'Paul Newman apologizes every night this week – Channel 9.' This, of course, only served to intrigue and the viewing rating reached a record high.

However, in other ways this miserable début was not a wasted experience. Newman was determined that he would somehow retrieve himself from the disaster. During the weeks of filming he had been obliged to partake in Hollywood life and had happened on like minds, the new breed of actors from New York, many of whom were as disillusioned as himself. One such was the legendary James Dean, Hollywood's unwilling new discovery. Newman had met him briefly in New York and now the two occasionally shared a drink together, discussing the Hollywood nightmare. Dean was even more contemptuous of the film capital than Newman. He attracted an odd assortment of disciples, bit-players, ex-cons, cultists, whom he regaled with his fury and distaste at the industry. They hung on to his every word. 'Who am I trying to convince?' he once demanded after a particularly vitriolic tirade, 'Give any one of them a hundred bucks and they'd lick Jack Warner's ass.'

Newman took invaluable advice from some of the more steadfast survivors of the business. He became friendly with Kirk Douglas, with whom he would always remain close. Douglas had succeeded in retaining his professional integrity, insisting on signing only single-picture contracts. The only occasion he had broken his rule was with Warners on *Champion*, the film that turned him into a star. To obtain his release he did a picture with them for nothing.

Douglas advised Newman: 'To survive you must develop a kind of awareness of what it's all about and, hopefully, you also develop compassion. That happens when you realize that nobody is a genius. They're just talented people, some with more talent than others, working in a medium where occasionally things come together and the rest is due to luck, pal. Only then can you take off . . .'

Inspired despite his present ignominy, Newman determined to fight hard for roles that were of value and worthwhile. But he would never, in James Dean's words, 'lick ass'.

Despite superficial evidence to the contrary, this was an interesting period in Hollywood, though it was still run by Warner, Zanuck, Selznick, Cohn, Louis B. Mayer and Cecil B. De Mille, all of whom ruled with an iron hand in an iron glove. But there was a change in the air, a restlessness. This was the pre-transition period before the industry opened up and was forever altered.

The rebels were already here, and they were conquering. These were the best of the New York school of talent, men and women like Marlon Brando, Geraldine Page, Montgomery Clift, James Dean and Julie Harris. To established Hollywood society they were anarchists, troublemakers and eccentrics. At the same time Hollywood was committed to accommodating them. They had begun to represent big money at the box office.

The time was ripe for an actor of Newman's talents, but meanwhile he was forced to suffer the indignities of *The Silver Chalice*. Luckily, there was an agreement in his contract that permitted him to do two plays in New York. During filming he frantically urged his agent to find him

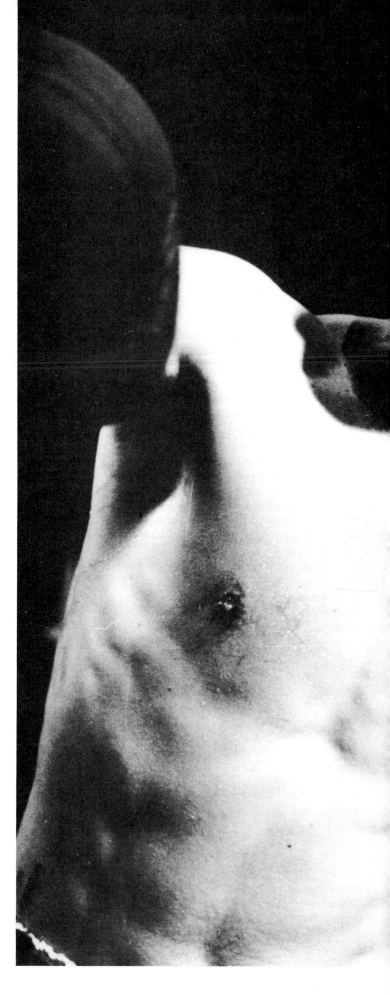

24

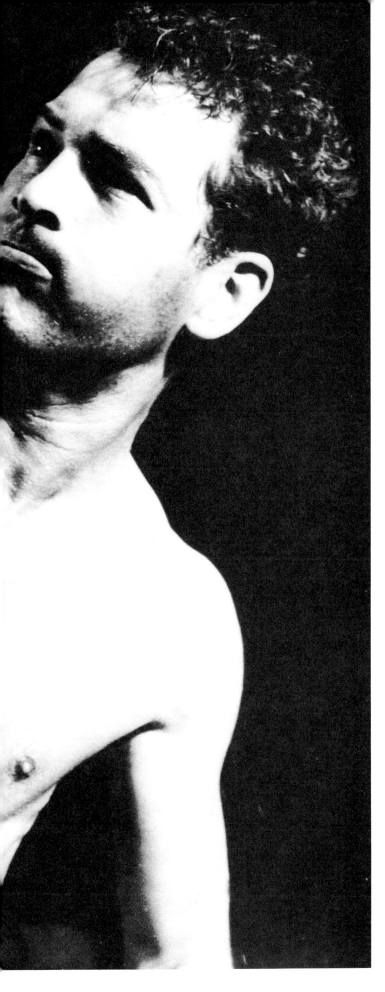

work in the New York theatre. Rightly, he felt that a good play might soften the blow of his inevitable failure in his first film. His prayers were answered when he was offered the role of Glan Griffin in *The Desperate Hours*, the part played by Humphrey Bogart in the later movie. Newman worked his last days out on *The Silver Chalice* almost with enthusiasm and had barely removed his make-up for the last time before he was on the plane to New York.

The play opened to glowing reviews and was a great success. It renewed Newman's flagging confidence. According to Robert Coleman of the *New York Daily Mirror*, the play 'pulled the firstnighters forward to the edge of their seats . . . ' Brooks Atkinson of the *New York Times* reported: 'Paul Newman plays the boss thug with a wildness that one is inclined to respect. The play shatters the nerves. There could be no more stir-crazy and animal-crafty desperado than Newman . . . ' John Chapman summed up: 'His is a splendid, tensely maniacal performance.' Broadway toasted its new star and the female adulation that was to become a permanent feature of his life was unloosed. A horde of teenage girls besieged their hero nightly at the stage door.

The play ran for eight months during which time *The Silver Chalice* was released. Newman's performance in *The Desperate Hours* did indeed qualify the disastrous impression he made in the film, although nothing could cure his humiliation at appearing in such a débâcle. The picture was a total flop and the unanimously unfavourable reception can be summed up by the damning words of John McCarten in the *New Yorker* magazine: 'As the Greek sculptor, Paul Newman, a lad who resembles Marlon Brando, delivers his lines with the emotional fervour of a Putnam Division conductor announcing local steps.'

Newman did not see *The Silver Chalice* until some of his friends dragged him to a cinema during the Philadelphia run of *The Desperate Hours*. They braced him with alcohol for the ordeal of the screening and Newman watched himself through a dismal, drunken haze of self-disgust.

Meanwhile, in New York, he continued twice-weekly classes at the Actors' Studio and worked in television. 'It was an exciting time for television,' says Newman. 'Young, talented writers wrote one-hour dramas for producers like those from the U.S. Theatre Guild.' He received critical acclaim for his performances in *Bang the Drum Slowly* and *The Five Fathers of Pepe*. 'Television was exciting because it was live,' continues Newman. 'Men like Tad Mosel and Paddy Chayefsky and Max Shulman were writing for television and they made it an inventive era. Call it Kitchen Sink, inner search, what you will – it was great . . . That whole glorious period has disappeared.' At the time American television was not solely the advertisers' medium that it has since become. Drama played regularly and good actors and actresses regarded these as the next best to a stage performance.

As a result of *The Silver Chalice*'s financial failure, Newman had to accept a modification to his Warner's contract. As well as the two films a year over five years, the studio would also have the option of a third. Having totally bound Newman by contract, Warners did not quite know what to do with their unsuccessful protégé. They finally

Somebody Up There Likes Me, 1956

resolved the problem by lending him out to Metro-Goldwyn-Mayer Studios, where Dora Shaw agreed to buy part of his contract. Metro cast Newman in his second film, *The Rack*, in which he played a young officer accused of having collaborated with the Communists during the Korean war. He felt happy with the part and delivered a fine performance, while the film itself was well received by the critics.

A sad stroke of fate engineered the next important move in Newman's career. On 30 September 1955, his old acquaintance James Dean was killed in a horrific motor accident. Newman was devastated. Only a few weeks later he was to have started work with Dean in a television adaptation of Ernest Hemingway's *The Battler*. Dean was to have played 'the battler', while Newman had been cast as Nick Adams. When Dean died, Newman's first instinct was to have nothing more to do with the play. Then the directors and producers begged him to take over Dean's role, and he finally accepted. The role was that of a fighter who falls from the unbeatable champ of his twenties to the recalcitrant prison inmate in his thirties, and then to a punch-drunk bum at forty. Newman had to age from twenty to forty in one hour, and the shadow of Dean haunted him throughout the production. It was a taxing, exhausting role, but he was superb in the part.

The Battler was transmitted coast to coast. After the showing Fred Coe, the producer, took Newman out for a drink and most of the rest of the cast joined them; the mood was celebratory and slightly tipsy. Suddenly an extremely small man, who had just seen Newman as 'the battler', took it upon himself to challenge the actor. Although small, this contender managed to cause considerable damage in the brawl that followed. At the end of the fracas, Newman's face was bruised and swollen and he sported a prize black eye.

The very next day, by which time his wounds had become even more colourful, Newman was invited to meet the director, Robert Wise, and his producer. Wise had seen *The Battler* and had been impressed by Newman's performance.

Now again, Newman's fate was linked to James Dean's death. Wise and his producer, Charles Schnee, had been planning a film on the life of the heavyweight boxer, Rocky Graziano, and decided on Dean for the role. Newman was their first thought as a replacement. The actor's appearance, however, caused some alarm to the assembled company when he arrived. Newman recalls the occasion: 'I walked into the office wearing an eye shade underneath a pair of dark glasses. There were several important people in the office and my entrance caused a bit of a stir. "What's happened?", the producer asked, "Why are you wearing that shade and those glasses?" I said: "You know where I got in the show last night?" There was a lot of nodding of heads. They had all seen the telecast of the play. "Well, we put a bit too much realism into it – and this is the result." '

'Boy,' Charles Schnee remarked, 'you show real dedication, kid.' And Newman got the part. The film was *Somebody Up There Likes Me*.

It was the role that Newman had been waiting for. This was a jewel of a part, right for the times, right for him. 'Rebel' films were then at the height of their vogue, conflict between the generations preoccupied 1950s America, and the 'bad boy made good' was a folk hero of the contemporary life.

Graziano's life embraced these current attitudes. Newman could not wait to start.

For days before filming, Newman spent from every morning till night with Graziano. He studied the fighter's speech, gestures, mannerisms and peculiarities. He watched him box, how his body moved, and where his strength lay. The fighter and the actor talked in depth about Graziano's early life, his relationship with his drunken father, and the ethos of the deprived neighbourhood in which he was raised and survived. By the time Newman embarked on the second phase of his preparation for the role, being taught how to box, he had a precise idea of the character he was to portray. Knowing how to play the part authentically, now began the relentless physical training necessary to bring a similar reality to the action scenes. Working out at the Hollywood Gym, he was soon in peak condition. Between sessions he would spar with professional boxers. He had never looked better.

Newman put everything he had into perfecting his portrayal of Rocky. When shooting finally began there was no holding him. Robert Wise was renowned as a director who understood how to bring out the best in his artists. The combination of Newman's talent and dedication with Wise's tactful control, and tight grasp of the material, produced a masterful result. At last Newman discovered that making films could be a joy, a true fulfilment.

Somebody Up There Likes Me was released in the summer of 1956 to rave reviews, with Newman singled out for special praise. *Variety*'s Brog echoed the consensus of opinion: 'For Paul Newman *Somebody Up There Likes Me* is a showcasing that should remove the Brando look-alike handicap. His talent is large and flexible.'

Comparisons with Brando had long been a constant irritant to Newman. While it would be some time before the tag would disappear, *Somebody Up There Likes Me* was the film which established a unique identity for him. With the public, the picture brought him stardom overnight. He was hotly in demand in career terms and also for himself.

Meanwhile home was still centred on Jackie in Long Island. By now Scott and Susan had been joined by a second daughter, Stephanie, born in 1955. For Jackie, her husband's runaway success was hard to adapt to, although it was what she had always wanted for him. Newman's two lives, one that of the successful, fêted actor, the other the family man, co-existed uneasily. The two had married young, then Jackie had renounced the professional world which they had shared at meeting. Three small children took up much of her time. They were a couple who loved each other and their children. Life should have been good.

But perhaps such huge success had come too fast. At a time when he should have been celebrating his good fortune, Newman did not *feel* good. He was not at ease within himself; he seethed with conflict.

From all sides he was under pressure, publicly, privately, and on the battlefield of his own emotions. He detested Hollywood yet he knew that he must stay there. In a single jolt of fortune he had been thrust forward to become a star. He was famous and he was wanted – but he was not at all sure that he liked what it was doing to him inside.

With Pier Angeli in Somebody Up There Likes Me

4
JOANNE

Paul Newman's first marriage was a good one. His affection for Jackie had not diminished with success or the arrival of three babies. He adored his children. Jackie was intelligent, mature and understood her husband well. She had been the first to recognize and appreciate his potential.

It is a tragic fact of life, however, that in unique and exceptional circumstances even this is not enough. Although a sensitive man, Paul Newman was nevertheless possessed of a large ego. A characteristic of many successful actors, the trait is often objectionable, though this has never been the case with Newman. But there had always been the charm and a strong desire to attract attention. Thwarted for so long, as he became successful his confidence grew and, along with it, so did his personality. His presence filled the spaces he inhabited. That elusive gift, 'star quality', always apparent to some, now shone forth to all. He dominated an atmosphere without effort or self-consciousness.

Jackie, on the other hand, had given up her own career, an understandable move. She yielded graciously to her more charismatic and talented husband, because life would have been intolerable for their children had both pursued their ambitions in that profession. Quite apart from that, she enjoyed the role of wife and mother. And she had always guessed that Newman would one day become successful.

As Newman's career prospered, as his circle of friends grew wider and more interesting, Jackie's world remained centred on her home and family. It was not that she had become dull or unadventurous. She was well-liked and admired for her qualities. But she had three growing children who needed constant attention if they were to be brought up in the way she and their father believed to be correct. The unfair fact of the matter was that Jackie was simply not in the position to keep up with her husband's life. It was nobody's fault. It was possible that she and the children should have travelled more with Newman. On the other hand, there was as much chance of her feeling an outsider if she had been seen merely an appendage to the star.

It is a sad process when one partner moves ahead of the other. These two liked and respected each other without equivocation but a chasm had appeared between them, unwelcome to both. They simply shared less in common. Jackie, his first champion, had been replaced by others with more to offer than mere advice. Tension mounted and both were aware of a foreboding difficult to articulate. This uncomfortable sense of something brewing, undefined yet destructive, is a feeling only those who have been there can understand. It is an unpleasant and painful experience, a kind of ghastly waiting game.

How the eruption finally occurred was, on the surface, a typical Hollywood cliché. Beneath the surface, however, it was untypical; there were no public recriminations, no desertions, no hatred, or revenge money involved. All the individuals in the drama cared a great deal about each other and their feelings.

Soon after Newman had moved to Los Angeles, Joanne Woodward landed a contract with 20th Century Fox. The two, friends since *Picnic*, spent more time together than was healthy for the Newman marriage. Their liking for each other grew until it was impossible for either to avoid the fact that they were in love.

Affairs, infidelity and the inevitable deceits did not come easy to a man like Newman. He could not take them lightly. At heart he was a one-woman man. His whole upbringing, the whole ethos of what he had been brought up to believe

Joanne Woodward

in, was contrary to the concept of divorce and the break-down of family life. At the same time he was unable to deny his feelings towards Miss Woodward. He was lost, he felt miserable without her.

His dilemma was excruciating. At a time when he should have been enjoying success, he found himself more unhappy than he had ever been.

Joanne Woodward was born on 27 February 1930 in the small town of Thomasville, Georgia. As a child she was the victim of a broken home. Her father, Wade Woodward, an intelligent, attractive man who later became vice-president of the publishers Scribner's was divorced by Joanne's mother during the small girl's early years. The event affected Joanne deeply. She adored her father. Once he had left she rarely saw him, and she missed him acutely throughout her childhood. Divorce became anathema to her and it was due to her own experiences that, later, she was able to feel so much sympathy for the Newman family.

She was brought up by her mother, spending her child-hood and youth in the South. What distinguished her was her intelligence – her I.Q. rating was, and is, dauntingly high. At high school she was already keenly interested in acting. Unlike Newman, Miss Woodward had been certain of her course from early on. As a child she had seen Greer Garson in a film on the life of Madame Curie. Inspired, for a short while she thought of becoming a doctor but soon reali-zed that it was the acting in the film, rather than its subject, that had touched her. There was another moment, one of unparalleled excitement, when, at the age of nine, she saw Vivien Leigh at the Southern World Première of *Gone With the Wind*. Joanne's mother retains the memory of that day: 'She was so excited, she kept jumping up and down in her seat when Vivien Leigh, as Scarlett O'Hara, came on the screen. Joanne would point her finger at her and tell me in a stage whisper, "I shall be a great actress one day." You know something? She was so convincing I was ready to believe her even then, though she wasn't anywhere near ten years old. She was always gifted with a vivid imagination but highly intelligent with it.'

Above: Joanne and Nell with Susan, Newman's eldest daughter from his first marriage to Jackie Witte

Left: Mr and Mrs Newman with firstborn, Nell

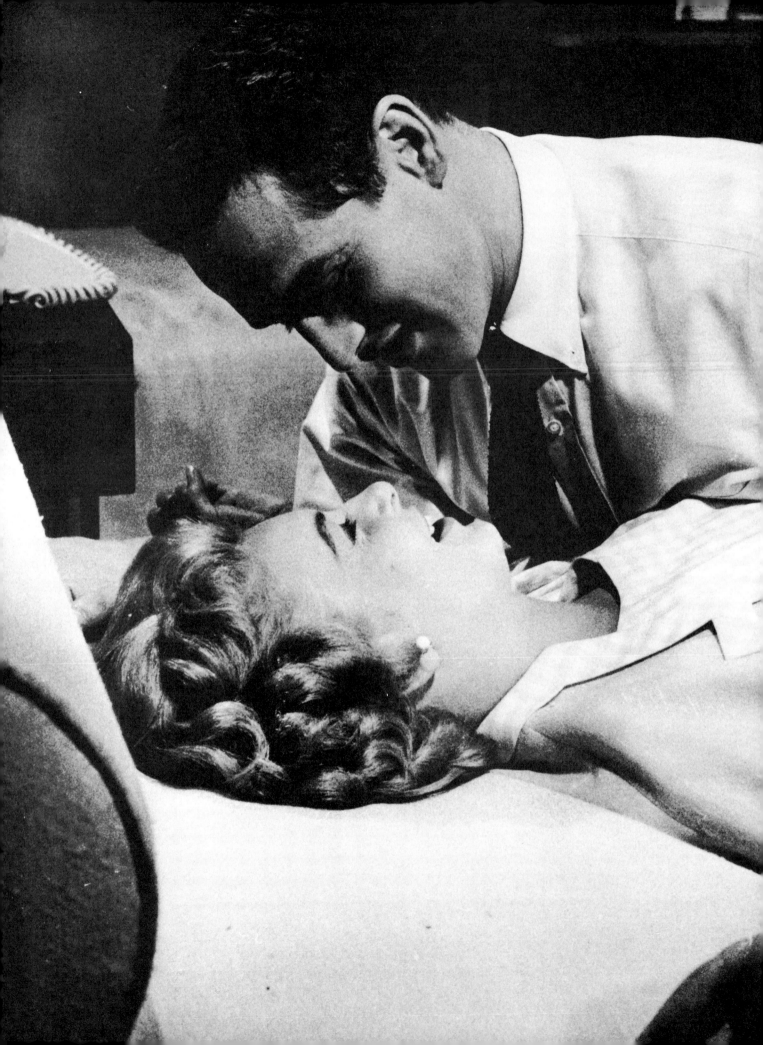

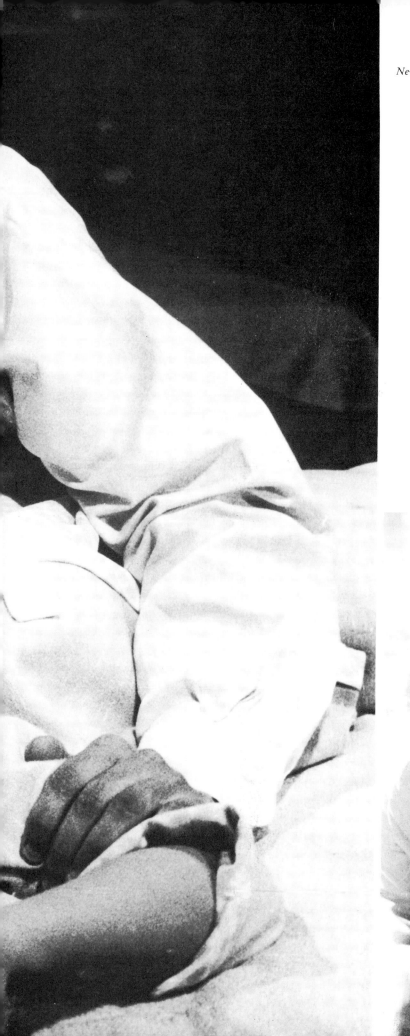

Newman and Joanne in From the Terrace, *1960*

Miss Woodward spent two years at the University of Louisiana before persuading her parents to allow her to move to New York for drama courses. Once there, she enrolled at the Actors' Studio and made a few television appearances before becoming understudy to the roles of both Janice Rule and Kim Stanley in *Picnic*.

Her career moving parallel to Newman's, Joanne entered films, signing with 20th Century Fox. From the start she was adamant about the way in which this career should be managed, refusing to act out the publicity pin-up/starlet charade. Many intelligent Hollywood actresses before her, such as Frances Farmer and Hildegarde Neff, had been destroyed by such non-conformity. Hollywood responded badly to individualists, automatically labelling them 'troublemakers'. But such was the power and effect of Miss Woodward's forceful argument that even the most feared studio bosses were known to yield. She usually succeeded in getting her own way and, more often than not, it was the right one.

By the time she renewed her friendship with Newman, Joanne was on the brink of a successful career, having been cast in the three roles of *The Three Faces of Eve*. The Newman she met in Hollywood, like her, had already fulfilled some of the dreams they had shared in New York.

Their attraction for each other had many facets. Apart from the fact that Miss Woodward's childhood had been less happy and secure than Newman's, the two had much in common. Both came from comfortable backgrounds, both had demonstrated their acting abilities at college, both had studied at the Actors' Studio and landed film contracts. Miss Woodward was on a par with Newman, equally successful and every bit as clever. She was a constant spur and inspiration. Both aware of the pressures of success, they understood each other well. Neither swamped the other as so often happens when two competitive, highly talented people join in a relationship. Also, Miss Woodward was as much in love with Newman as he was with her.

At the same time Newman was still deeply attached to his wife and grateful for the love and support she had given him throughout the years. He had three children for whom not only did he feel responsible but needed.

He was torn between his painful choices. The fact was that he and Joanne were made for each other. Joanne was not 'better' than Jackie, it was simply that she was his natural soul-mate.

Above: Joanne with daughter Melissa, 1978

Left: Daughter Claire, with Joanne seated right, 1973

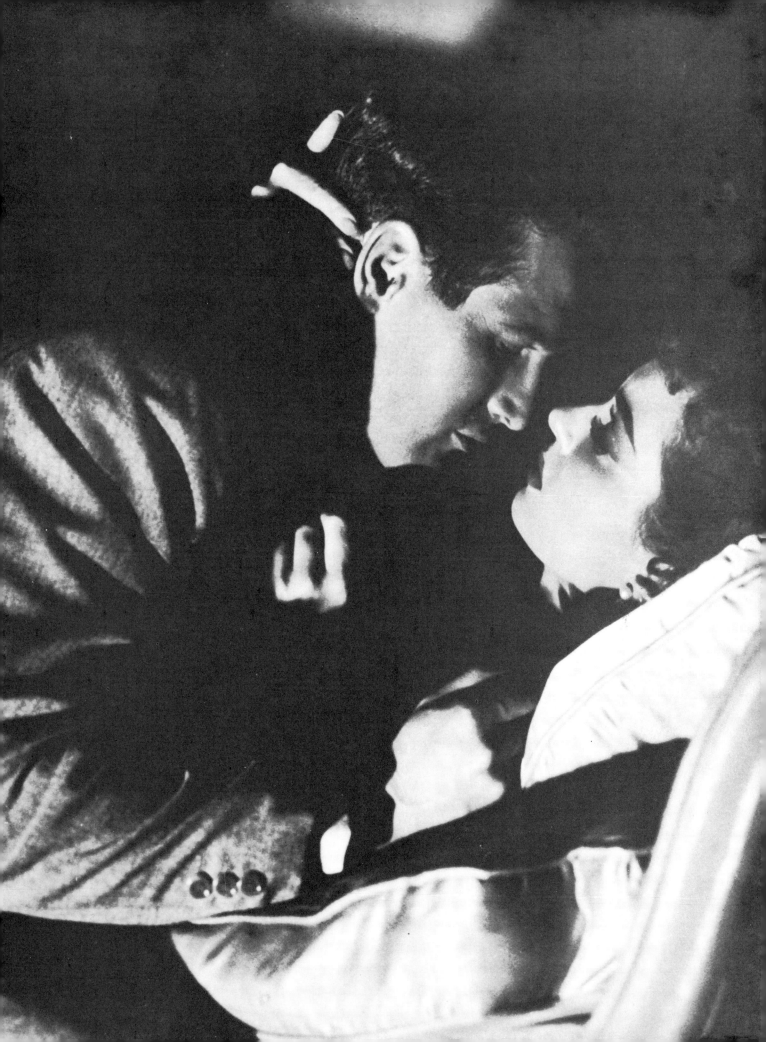

Page 36: With Jean Simmons on the set of Until They Sail, *1957*

Page 37: The Helen Morgan Story *with Anne Blyth, 1957*

Below: Joanne with daughter Melissa at the Emmy Awards ceremony, 1978

But it would be some time before they could enjoy happiness together without guilt. Their concern for others caused them more than the usual despair experienced in such crisis.

Joanne was a tactful young woman and, like Jackie, strong and sensitive. It was intolerable to her to become the centre of a public scandal in the role of *femme fatale*, the homebreaker. She and Newman decided not to see each other again – Paul would return to his family; it was not as though his marriage had deteriorated into hatred and contempt and it would be a serious injustice to deny a father to the growing children.

It is easy to imagine how agonizing this decision was for everyone concerned – Joanne losing the man unique in her affections; Jackie at a precarious advantage yet acutely aware of how much her husband missed the actress; and Newman himself torn between two women whom he loved.

With such emotional demands upon him it was difficult for Newman to take pleasure in his profession. In this, too, he felt cornered – since *Somebody Up There Likes Me* he had been obliged by contract to appear in mediocre projects that filled him with distaste. For the first time in the Golden Boy's life just about everything had gone wrong. He became troublesome, and difficult to be with. An earlier incorrect comparison to Brando now seemed true. Moody and introverted, he drank more. He became aggressive and – totally out of character – would sometimes instigate a fight at minimal provocation. He remained in Hollywood, leaving Jackie and the children in Long Island. But he never saw Joanne during this time.

The drinking became so serious that it got him into real trouble. The problem reached its crisis one hot summer night on a trip back home to Long Island. On 7 July 1956, he was arrested on charges of drunken driving. He had left the scene of an accident, racing through a red light. He was so drunk that he attempted to fight off his captors singlehandedly, and they finally were obliged to handcuff and slap him in jail. At Mineola police station Newman was abusive, telling the officer in charge, 'I'm acting for Rocky Graziano, beat it!' Patrolman Rocco Caggiano came back, 'Yeah, and I'm Rocky too, and you're under arrest, pal.' Newman spent the night in a cell and woke up with a hangover, embarrassment and severe remorse.

At this low point in his life there was one haven that remained to him. Whenever he was in New York, Newman continued as a student at the Actors' Studio. Its discipline sustained him and in the understanding personality of Lee Strasberg he found solace from a world turned harsh and sharp-edged. Studying and learning among friends his problems fell into a sort of perspective. He was alarmed by the uncontrollable side of his personality, his *alter ego* become flesh and blood.

Seen from the viewpoint of the Actors' Studio the work he was doing in Hollywood appeared particularly ignoble. By now he had started on his fourth film, *Until They Sail*, a sentimental tale of women left behind in war. It was a dismal come-down after *Somebody Up There Likes Me*.

Under the terms of his contract Newman was obliged to accept any assignment Warner Brothers gave him. They could hire him to other studios and had only to rent out their discontented star to turn a handsome profit on their investment. He remembers, 'They were still paying me a

Right: Newman and Joanne with his daughter, Susan

straight $1,000 a week while hiring me out for a few weeks' work at $75,000 a time. There was no possibility of my getting even a small percentage of the profits.'

In that same year of 1957 Newman had starred in yet another undistinguished Warner vehicle, *The Helen Morgan Story*. In this cliché-bound film he played the part of a gangster who turns over a new leaf. Superficially, it was a typical Newman role, a man from the wrong side of the tracks, hustling to make good in spite of it. But the script was poor: ' . . . in my own way, Helen, I love you.' The main character had little depth and it became yet another of those films that he later tried to forget he had ever made.

Newman's salary had to cover a wide range of expenses: agent's fees, business and legal fees, and the considerable cost of commuting from coast to coast, from work to family, and back again. This was something he had expressly chosen to do. He could not conceive of his children growing up in Hollywood to become spoiled and old before their time. So Jackie and the children remained on Long Island.

Meanwhile he could not help but be constantly aware of his lost love. Joanne Woodward's name was all over Holly-

wood. Word had it that her performance in *The Three Faces of Eve* was so good as to be astonishing; if the promise visible in the rushes could be sustained she would be a serious contender for an Oscar. Newman was not allowed to forget her, even had he wanted to.

Though the critics dismissed *Until They Sail* and *The Helen Morgan Story* both pictures were successful at the box office. While *Somebody Up There Likes Me* had shown him to be a star, these trite little films confirmed him as a money-spinner. He continued to be in demand.

Meanwhile, fortunately, the old Shaker Heights values came to the aid of the reluctant movie star. Common sense prevailed. Newman faced up to the fact that if he was to lose self-control and allow his emotions to run haywire, not only would he make others unhappy, his career would suffer too. The old resolve returned. He would not allow his weaknesses to jeopardize his career. Self-destruction was not really in Newman's blood. Stubbornness, rebelliousness, yes, but at heart he believed in himself. He was determined not to become an alcoholic. He had lived in a thoughtless and reckless manner for quite long enough. The wayward

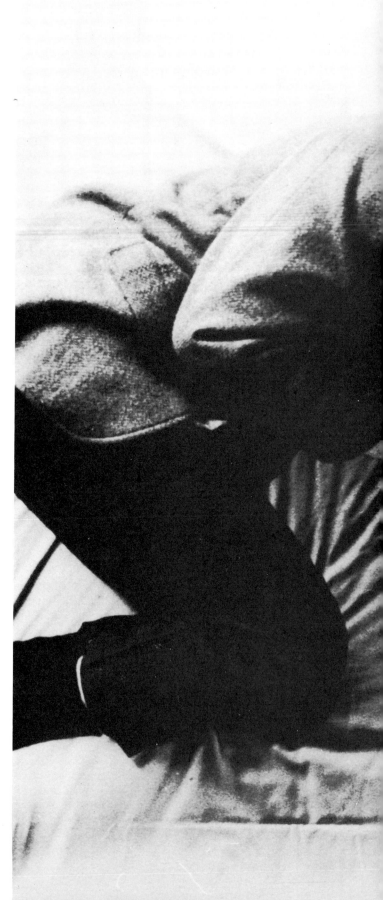

life was meaningless and solved no problems, it merely exacerbated them. He knew he was a better man than that. He began calmly to take stock of his life and for the first time in months took a practical step towards resolving the conflict in himself.

Discreetly, not wishing to set unrealistic store upon its possibilities, he consulted an analyst. He had come a long way in ten years in terms of understanding himself and his fellow men. He recognized that he was a mass of contradictions and confusions and regarded the help of an analyst as a natural and practical step towards putting his mind in order. He did not consider the decision a major one. Rather, he regarded analysis as a kind of business deal. If there was a mess, it needed to be cleared up. If the mess happened to be emotional, there were defined and methodical ways of sorting this out.

As it happened, analysis not only helped him sort out his current problems, it turned out to be a rewarding experience. He says of the process: 'what measure of serenity I have in my life is a direct result of analysis. It brought me every possible benefit. My acting improved and I achieved a greater control of myself . . . People should not be afraid of it. Anything you can do to develop a realistic appraisal of yourself is immensely useful . . . Analysis is always interesting. You never stop learning. It's never really finished . . .'

Newman is a man always totally committed to what he embraces, whether this be acting, analysis, a hobby, a sport, or a new idea. On one occasion, realizing any serious discussion of the topic must need be backed by facts, he set himself upon a six-week crash programme to learn everything about atomic weapon tests, fall-out, nuclear war, retaliation, defence and the chances of survival. He read everything available on the subject and sought out experts in the field to explain yet more to him. It is this same fervour which is put to use in his work. Before he plays a character whose experiences he has not known directly, he will spend weeks living and dissecting those experiences, seeking out the feel and essence of the places from which that character derives.

With analysis, Newman soon came to regard his life in better perspective. His private life was as chaotic as ever, his career still a disappointment, but he began to view the whole more healthily. The compulsion to escape through drink diminished and then largely disappeared.

It was inevitable, of course, in that incestuous world that Newman and Woodward's paths would cross from time to time. Despite their resolve they started to see each other again.

During that time, as if fate finally decided the course of the affair, Joanne's studio 20th Century Fox, were searching for an actor for the lead in the film of William Faulkner's *The Long Hot Summer*. Newman was chosen for the role and, once again, was loaned out from Warner's. The part, that of the character Ben Quick, was a good one. But there was another reason that made this production attractive to Newman.

The role of his co-star, that of an innocent young Southern girl, was given to Joanne Woodward. For the first time the lovers would be together in the same picture. The magic that existed between them would now be witnessed by

HORSES

the world at large – including Jackie who, with the best will in the world, could only have felt humiliated.

The film was to be shot on location in Clinton, Mississippi. As was by now his habit, Newman travelled down before the rest of the crew to get a feel for the atmosphere of his character. Spending his days hanging out in bars and pool rooms, he listened to people talking, taking note of their accents and mannerisms. For a while no one knew who he was. He was completely accepted.

When the crew arrived his cover was blown, of course, but he had so endeared himself to the locals that he remained popular with them throughout filming. Some of the 'tough guys' of the area showed their loyalty in a touching manner. The romance between Newman and Miss Woodward was still considered to be hot gossip in Hollywood and when a reporter turned up, snooping for tit-bits, the town's young bloods rounded on him in a bar one night. Roughing him up just a little, they persuaded the journalist to leave town.

Newman and Woodward worked marvellously together. The experience exposed another exhilarating aspect to their relationship. Not only did they share a unique love, they could also create together. There could be no more doubts as to whether they should be together. Their commitment was sealed during those long, hot days in Missouri.

And it was Jackie, realizing what had happened, who took the final decision into her own hands. The whole experience, particularly this latest episode, had been painful and humiliating for her yet, without malice, revenge, or public spectacle of the woman scorned, she filed for divorce with the minimum of fuss. She had always understood Newman well, and no less did she understand his needs now. It would have been more than comprehensible had she chosen at this unhappy time to withhold her compassion, saving her energies for her own life. But she did not. There had been enough fighting and hurting. She gave in with dignity, making the break as painless to the children as was possible. They were not unmarked by their parents' divorce, but they never felt or saw hatred. They were not threatened by the sense that they might lose either parent's love and affection. Used to their father's absences through work, they continued to see almost as much of him as before.

The storm was over and Newman was at last free to marry Miss Woodward. They settled for a modest ceremony in Las Vegas in January 1958.

The couple honeymooned in England. They went first to London and stayed at the Connaught, one of the most civilized and unpretentious hotels in the world. Here they met old and new friends like the Ustinovs, the Ken Tynans and Laurence Olivier.

They moved on, travelling to Scotland. They walked, sat in pubs and talked to people, unconstrained and enjoying the life of ordinary people.

It was a good time. Newman was on the threshold of a new life, married to a woman he knew he would be with for the rest of his days. He would never quite recover from the guilt at the failure of his first marriage but he also knew he had found where he belonged.

'Without her,' he says of Miss Woodward, 'I'd be nowhere – nothing.'

Susan congratulates Joanne after the opening of Candida *on Broadway in 1981*

Following pages: A marriage of true minds: at home shortly, after their marriage

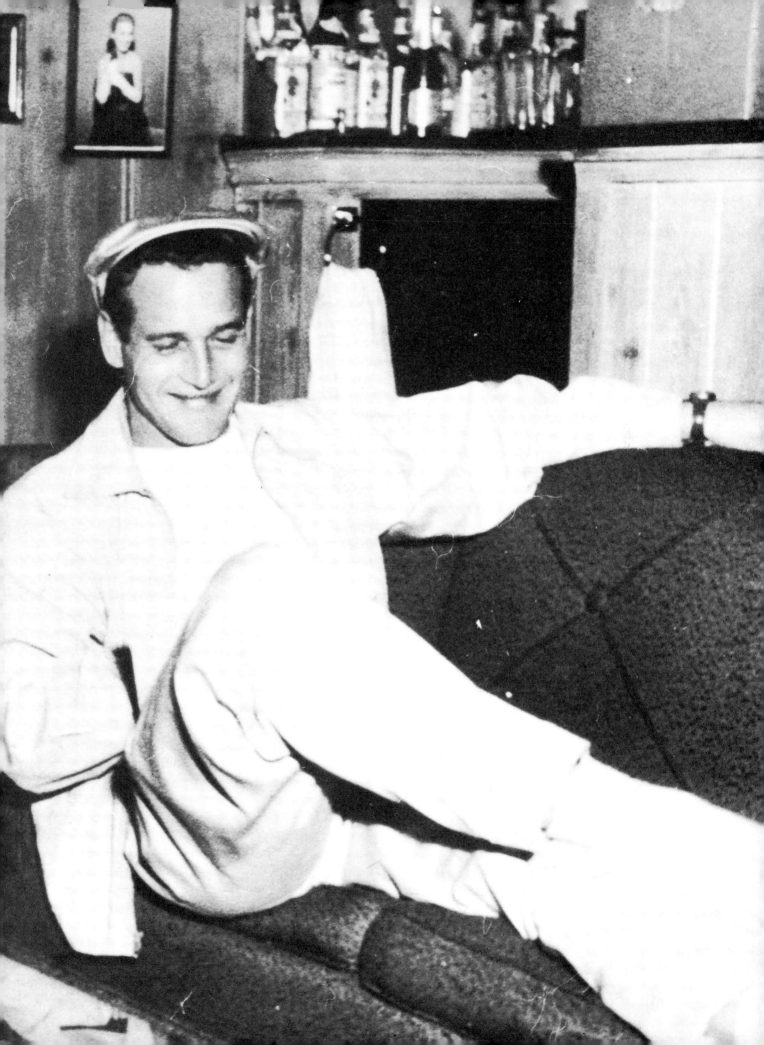

5
GLITTERING PRIZES

When the Newmans returned from England they rented a flat in an old apartment house in New York's East Eighties. While not everyone's idea of a movie star's residence, it was nevertheless comfortable and tastefully decorated with sufficient space for the children when they visited – and for any additions to the family. It boasted a few fine pieces of furniture, including a vast brass bed bought from a New Orleans brothel.

The couple had every reason to be delighted with life in that year of 1958. Apart from their personal happiness with each other, both had recently received honours representing the seal of approval of their profession. Newman had gained Best Actor Award at the Cannes Film Festival for his performance in *The Long Hot Summer*, the first American to have been so chosen. Joanne had won the Oscar as Best Actress of 1957 for her part in *The Three Faces of Eve*. The predictions during filming on her first major and treble role had come true.

Here was a golden couple, young, beautiful, talented and successful. They were popular, sought-after and well-liked. Their happiness was complete when Joanne became pregnant that same year. Meanwhile Jackie had skilfully and tactfully guided their three children through the trauma of divorce. They knew that their father's new marriage in no way affected his love for them, Scott, Susan and Stephanie visited frequently and stayed in what they accepted as their second home, and they grew to adore their stepmother.

During that eventful year Newman starred in *The Left-Handed Gun* as Billy the Kid. Like the role of Rocky Graziano, this particular interpretation of Billy fitted Newman's talents perfectly and was an indication of the distinctive parts for which he would become renowned.

The Left-Handed Gun was based on Gore Vidal's tele-play, *The Death of Billy the Kid*. He and Newman had become close friends since their early days in Hollywood and Vidal had gained a reputation for his sharp, original style, clever, witty and acerbic. It was an unusual friendship. While both men shared a privileged background – Vidal's even more than Newman's – they were opposites in many ways. Newman was the straight family man now and, although he could never suffer fools gladly, his manner was neither cynical nor anarchic. Vidal, on the other hand, was a complicated man, a bachelor, no lover of domestic life and a self-confessed bisexual. The two appeared to have very little in common. Yet the Newmans were so fond of Vidal that they later chose him as godfather to their daughter. His incisive, cultured mind cut straight to the heart of things. Recklessly courageous in this views, he disdained the consequences. Newman admired such qualities; he was stimulated by intelligence and intellectual excellence.

Vidal's attraction to Newman – and to his wife – is easily understood. He had once been engaged to Miss Woodward – a sure sign of esteem, since he was hardly the marrying kind. Superficially, he liked the Newmans because they were attractive and successful – in a word, glamorous. But more deeply, as a man despising cant and hypocrisy, he admired their straightforwardness, their stability and their facility for truth, rare attributes in the world of show business.

The Newmans maintained a friendship with other so-called 'odd-balls', such as Tennessee Williams, Anthony Perkins and the late Laurence Harvey, and other lesser-known characters had, and have, a place within their circle. Newman is interested in people *per se*; he is attracted to those who have something to offer, or who possess a talent, whether they be successful or not. Neither of the Newmans had any need to climb a social ladder and neither is socially discriminating or snobbish.

Newman was enthusiastic about playing the part of Billy as characterized by Vidal. However, because the hero was depicted as a neurotic, almost psychopathic adolescent, the film was difficult to mount. But Newman was committed and adamant. He and Joanne were becoming known as pioneers, fighters for their ideals, and both were fearless of the risks implicit in their stand. Inevitably, they made enemies in the industry.

In the face of opposition and difficulty, the film finally was made. Newman's portrayal of Billy expressed all the

Left: With Joanne at a gala in honour of both of them at the Film Society of Lincoln Center, 1975

intensity of a confused, forceful and uneducated character. He and director Arthur Penn established an excellent rapport and the actor's performance was sensitive and impeccable. The film was not a great success at the box office, however, and many disliked Newman's interpretation. The public were not yet ready to accept a hero – or anti-hero – who differed so radically from the conventional Western legend. Even such intelligent Westerns as *Shane* and *High Noon*, both of which had broken traditional barriers in this genre, retained the time-honoured theme of the 'good guy' versus the 'bad guy'.

Many critics considered the film too off-beat, and reviews differed widely. Howard Thompson of the *New York Times* wrote harshly: 'The sad thing is that some T.V. people have tried to make a Western that's different. And, by golly, it is . . . Poor Mr. Newman seems to be auditioning alternatively for the Moscow Art Players and Grand Old Opry as he ambles about, grinning or mumbling endlessly.' In contrast, *Variety* reported: 'A smart and exciting Western paced by Paul Newman's intense portrayal of the Kid. Newman dominates the picture.'

Though not a success in the conventional sense, the film was important, for it was before its time and seminal in form. Through playing Billy, Newman found confirmation of the kind of role he understands best. The precedent had been set with *Somebody Up There Likes Me. The Left-Handed Gun* established him in those rebellious, intricate roles he has made his own.

His reputation for this specialized excellence endorsed, Newman was now every producers' first choice for an anti-hero role. His next was a jewel: he was chosen for the part of Brick in the screen version of Tennessee Williams's *Cat On a Hot Tin Roof*. Newman's co-star as Brick's wife was the ultimate superstar and Oscar winner, Elizabeth Taylor.

In 1958 *Cat On a Hot Tin Roof* was considered a shocking and daring project. The plot revolves around the emotional life of a Southern family, dominated by a father (Big Daddy, played by Burl Ives) who does not know he is dying of cancer. Every member of his tribe is in conflict with themselves and others, and all are handicapped by inability to express their true feelings. Each suffers the consequences of his or her evasions until, in the final scenes, the lid blows off and the truth is told. The mother (Judith Anderson) sees a life of hypocrisy and deceit as the norm. Her thirty-year-old son, Brick, impotent and emotionally crippled, avoids his responsibilities by numbing himself with alcohol. Brick's wife, Maggie, strident and blousy, is the character most true to herself and prepared to take risks for the sake of sanity. The mood of the original play was heavy with tension, and Richard Brooks, co-writer and director of the film, managed to transfer this heat and pressure to the screen.

The picture was located in Mississippi. When filming began, the Press hung over the proceedings like vultures, for Miss Taylor, a fine actress, was the gossip columnist's dream. They hovered impatiently awaiting the scandals, the fights, the tantrums, the catastrophes they had come to expect. When the partnership between Newman and Taylor was announced, Hollywood shivered with delicious anticipation. Surely the handsome, blue-eyed sex symbol, at

Cat On a Hot Tin Roof, with Elizabeth Taylor, 1958

Page 50: Brick and Maggie the Cat

Page 51: The Newmans in Rally Round the Flag, Boys!, *1958. At the time comedy was not judged to be Newman's forte though later he was to prove his critics wrong*

Below: On the set of Rally Round the Flag, Boys! *with Joanne and Joan Collins*

his physical peak and looking marvellous, would not fail them this time? Newman's marriage was known to be among the most stable in show business and this rendered him a constant disappointment to the muckrakers. He never generated their kind of news. However, now faced with the prospect of long hot weeks with the luscious and fiery Elizabeth . . .

Of course, Newman disappointed them. He preferred to go home to his wife when his work was done. Miss Taylor, in any case, was then married to the one man who, of all her husbands, was most suited to her needs. Her union with Mike Todd was tempestuous and theatrical and neither was averse to airing their grievances in public – another reason why the columnists loved them. But, despite this tendency to brawl, the Mike Todds were completely and utterly involved in each other. Newman and Taylor's relationship would be strictly professional.

The result of their working partnership was stunning, all the more so in view of the tragedy that occurred during production. Halfway through filming Mike Todd was killed in an air crash in New Mexico. Elizabeth Taylor was devastated by the loss of the man she had loved so passionately. All her strength was needed to go on which the picture, and in this she was helped by Brooks and Newman. There is little doubt that their kindness and stability helped to support her throughout the remainder of filming. By the time the picture was completed she had delivered the best performance of her career.

Newman's acting was also his best to date. He transcended himself and caused Brick, with all his flaws, to come over as the most desirable of men.

The film was an enormous success at the box office and received six Oscar nominations, among them Newman's first as Best Actor and Miss Taylor's second as Best Actress. Some critics, however, did disapprove of the watering-down of Tennessee Williams's original play, and of director Richard Brooks' removal of the homosexual theme together with other nuances that had existed in the original Broadway play.

But for Newman it represented a considerable advance in terms of a distinctive screen image. His personal reviews were excellent and the film became the top money-spinner of 1958. *Variety* wrote of his performance: 'Newman again proves to be one of the finest actors in films, playing cynical underacting against highly developed action. His command of the articulate, sensitive sequences is unmistakable and the way he mirrors his feelings is basic to every scene.' Bosley Crowther in the *New York Times* summed up his notice: 'Mr Newman is perhaps the most resourceful and dramatically restrained of the lot. He gives an ingratiating picture of a tortured and tested young man.'

Although now in the big league, the Newmans avoided the usual show business haunts and gatherings. They were unlikely to be found at Sardi's or 21, preferring unpretentious restaurants of the kind frequented by still-struggling actors and actresses. Often they ate quietly at home, however, because by now it was impossible to appear in public without attracting attention. Almost everywhere they went a crowd would gather round, asking for autographs or simply staring.

Newman loathes this occupational hazard of his career. His privacy, and his indisputable right to it, are a major preoccupation of his life. He has never shown much sympathy for those who come up to him. These strangers, on the other hand, are his public, and dozens of more brazen and confident individuals, such as journalists, who have legitimately been at close range claim that it is simply impossible *not* to look at him, so striking is he to the eye. Thus one feels a certain sympathy for Joe Public in the aura of such magnetism.

At the same time Newman's life *is* seriously hampered by such unremitting attention and he and his wife have, from early on, lived in an unwelcome goldfish bowl. From the beginning he developed a technique in dealing with such avid curiosity. He behaves as if the problem did not exist. He signs no autographs these days and acts as naturally in public as if he were in his own back yard, carrying on with the business at hand, poised, at ease and, providing he is not harassed, displaying perfect manners. To onlookers, of course, this only makes him more attractive and compelling

to watch – the very ordinariness in one so famous seems extraordinary.

To escape from the pressures of the film world, the Newmans acquired a converted coaching-house in Connecticut soon after their marriage. Built in 1780, it possessed three acres of orchard and a trout stream. Here it was possible to mix with the local people who soon accepted the famous couple as themselves. At the time, such a move was regarded as capricious, even churlish, by the film community, who lived in huge security-protected houses close by other, like-minded neighbours in Los Angeles. The Newmans disliked that incestuous world and remained unmoved by criticisms that they shunned the very society that had made them what they were.

Whilst in New York, Newman, now in a position to ride in chauffeur-driven limousines, chose instead to travel around the city on a scooter. Togged out in cap and goggles he was unrecognizable and could move around freely, sometimes carrying Joanne on pillion.

Newman had everything he had ever wanted in life. His work, personal happiness and the security of financial success seemed to take the edge off his next couple of performances. It was almost as if the driving hunger had gone and he was resting on his laurels. His next film after *Cat On a Hot Tin Roof* was a comedy, *Rally Round the Flag, Boys!*, with Joanne as his co-star. In theory, the film had much going for it. Based on Max Schulman's humorous novel, its director and producer was the reputable Leo McCarey, a man who had proved himself in the field of comedy over a period of twenty-five years. Other top men also worked on the film – the photography and musical score were professional and first-rate. Despite this, the picture was not a success. By this time Newman had begun to gain a reputation for the roles he excelled in – difficult, moody, turbulent characters – and he was reprimanded by the critics for straying so far from his genre. In truth, comedy was not Newman's forte. In private, he is a man of wry humour but in this farce he overacted outrageously for laughs. However, the critics, who almost unanimously admired the actor, merely rapped his knuckles on this occasion and pointed out that he was no comedian.

Newman's next film was better but still the wrong vehicle for his talents. In *The Young Philadelphians*, the part he played was superficially in the right 'Newman' mode, that of a young lawyer from the wrong side of town, mean, hustling and devious. But this time direction and script did not complement the acting. Newman, however, just about carried the picture, as he has so often with mediocre projects, and was excused blame for its inadequacies. Laurence J. Quirk reported in *Screen Slants*: 'It's Mr. Newman who succeeds in making this picture more solid and craftsmanlike than it actually is. Who said film was primarily a *director's* medium?'

These lesser movies did not affect his financial situation adversely. Newman's status at Warners was high and his presence in a film commanded a high price. In August 1959 he was in a position to buy out his contract which still had three more years to run. It cost him $500,000, but he considered it well worth the price. At that time, as a free agent, he could ask for $200,000 a film – a vast improvement on the $25,000 he received for his contract films where

Warners simply pocketed all the considerable profits their star generated. Always a man to examine himself and his life objectively, Newman now reviewed his career with the heady luxury of a freedom he had not known for years.

He realized that he had grown complacent in Hollywood, that having learned to live with its standards on his own terms he had begun to lose his edge. While he still loathed the place as much as ever, to survive and succeed there as his own man had been a challenge. Having achieved his ends he had relaxed – an attitude apparent in his last two films.

He decided he must return to the hard graft of Broadway for a while. There he would be tried and tested once more by a live and critical audience, for better or worse. 'There's always that terrible fear,' he explains, 'that one day your fraud will be discovered and you'll be back in the dog kennel business. That's why it's good to work on Broadway as well as Hollywood. You know you'll get the hell kicked out of you here once in a while – but if you don't you'll fall back on a lot of successful mannerisms.'

He returned to the stage in a wildly successful production of Tennessee Williams's play *Sweet Bird of Youth*, which received the best notices of his career to date. He was right back on form. Brooks Atkinson wrote: 'The acting is magnificent . . . Newman's young man is the perfect centrepiece.' Robert Coleman in the *New York Daily Mirror* gave a glowing review, which ended: 'Newman, as well as the audience, was moved by the concluding passages of the play. There were tears in his eyes as well as in those of many outside.'

During these latest developments in her husband's career, Miss Woodward had also been busy. When she was pursuing her own career independently and not working with Newman she tended to play in only modestly successful pictures. In that same year she appeared in the lengthy *The Sound and the Fury* as a rebellious Southern girl, followed closely by a similar role in *The Fugitive Kind* with Marlon Brando. Miss Woodward – and she was only too aware of this – ran the risk of being typecast. She longed for diversity and the opportunity to enlarge her range. In that year 1959 an event occurred that temporarily soothed her artistic frustrations. Her first child by Newman, Elinor, was born.

After his prestigious success with *Sweet Bird of Youth* on Broadway, Newman's next film, his first as an independent actor, was a strange choice. It was a slick weepie, with the kind of script that Newman detested but, under contract, had been obliged to accept. *From the Terrace* was a poor story, although written by John O'Hara, and it is difficult to imagine why it caught Newman's fancy.

Once more he co-starred with his wife and the couple managed to bring the picture to some sort of life. But the dialogue was turgid and the whole production seemed contrived. In spite of this, like all Newman films since *The Long Hot Summer*, *From the Terrace* was a solid commercial success for, by this time, he was a sure-fire draw at the box office.

He was then offered the role of a Palestinian underground leader in an ambitious adaptation of Leon Uris's bestseller, *Exodus*. Directed by Otto Preminger, this three-and-a-half hour epic was regarded as a serious and prestigious undertaking within the business, and roles in the film were coveted by actors from all over the world.

The theme of the story, the founding of the State of Israel in 1947, was one which interested Newman deeply. With his Jewish blood, yet with no background in ritual or history, he was fascinated by the prospect of a role that would oblige him to learn and understand his origins.

He played the part of Ari Ben Canaan, who masterminds the successful escape of over 600 Jewish refugees from Cyprus to Palestine. The character faces a personal crisis when he falls in love with an American nurse and becomes close friends with a sympathetic Arab.

Thus when Newman travelled on location to Israel, followed by his wife and baby daughter, he was excited and enthusiastic about the project. As usual, he spent several weeks getting to know the country and its people. Seeing Israel for the first time felt like a kind of homecoming.

However, from the moment filming started, Newman was filled with misgivings. Preminger, though a director of repute, was a particularly tyrannical and arbitrary task-master. The film was headquartered in Haifa, and every possible facility had been laid on for the production which was vast and complex, involved many hundreds of people and was minutely scheduled to fit into a scant three-and-a-half months. The task of getting this epic made was daunting, and although Preminger was skilled with crowd and action scenes he was less gifted in his dealings with individuals. There was a lack of cohesion among those working on the film from the start, together with endless conflicts and petty battles over even the most minor problems.

All this resulted in an atmosphere of acute tension in which it was difficult for an actor to give of his best. There was also another problem for Newman. He had grown accustomed to discussing scripts, characters and changes with his directors, and he was respected by many for his intelligent contribution. Newman approached Preminger with some ideas but the director reacted negatively to his star's suggestions. It was an inauspicious start to a relationship that did not improve.

Nor was his difficulty unique. Ralph Richardson, Eva Marie Saint, Lee J. Cobb and Hugh Griffith, among others, were treated in a similar fashion. To add to the problems, the weather was hot, dry and windy, creating furthur irritation in a discontented cast and crew. Preminger dominated, oblivious to the human problems, demanding loyalty and total submission of all others' will.

In this uneasy atmosphere Newman did his best to give the character of Ari some depth and humanity – Ari, like so many Newman characters, was a single-minded loner, a type Newman was usually able to get to grips with easily. But the whole experience was depressing and unrewarding for everyone concerned and, even as he worked, Newman was aware of the defeated sense that he was delivering far below his best.

Whenever he had a free moment from the trials of filming, the Newmans would escape. They explored the country, taking in all that they could of its history and passing many days in Jerusalem.

There was a real-life tension in existence that made a nonsense of the squabbles on the set. Hatred was a palpable force that charged the air in troubled Israel. Antagonism and hostility were mounting in pressure towards their inevitable explosion. It was a passionate and violent world that Newman looked on and sometimes he detected a kind of shame in himself for being a mere actor of life rather than a

participant. This gloomy state of mind was not improved by the ever-growing troubles he encountered whenever he returned to filming.

Privately, the episode in Israel was important and interesting – as far as his career was concerned, however, it did nothing to re-establish Newman's strength as an actor.

The frustrations felt by all those involved in the production were reflected in the finished picture. *Exodus* was unanimously badly received by the critics and Newman's performance was described variously as 'wooden', 'lacking in warmth' and 'stiff'. Yet, paradoxically, *Exodus* grossed more at the box office than any other film Newman had been in up to that time and he received a handsome $200,000 for his part in the picture.

Even such an untidy, sprawling epic as *Exodus* could not harm his career now. Whatever he did, he had a loyal, enthusiastic audience. He was in demand. He was hot. Yet he required a critical success, a picture which would provide him with a vehicle for the unique ability that lay within him, that would confirm him as a star. He needed his definitive role.

The luck which attended his life was rapidly becoming a cliché. Now, once more, it stepped in to serve him well . . .

Above: Rehearsing From the Terrace

6
ALTER EGO

'I'm the son of a miserable Indian renegade who stole gasoline in the outbacks of Shaker Heights Reserve, Ohio . . .

'My mother was a poor invalid woman. I spent my days reading poetry. When my father died I started selling brushes. I was thirteen years old and the whole family lived off my earnings. On the day I was seventeen I ran away from home and signed up as a sailor on board an Iranian fishing boat . . .

'I lost my virginity at fourteen years old to a young Eskimo girl which is no doubt the reason, since that day, I've been a great lover of Eskimo food. I soon learned Speedy Gonzales' old trick of double parking in front of brothels and I never got a traffic violation. After that I was a lumberjack, drove a truck carrying nitro-glycerine, a great admirer of Brigitte Bardot, and one of the best popcorn makers in the country . . .

'Later on I was discovered by Erich von Stroheim, who was pretty old then. He recommended me enthusiastically to Walt Disney. The rest is history. I started doing the voices behind several animated films – I was Grumpy in *Snow White and the Seven Dwarfs*. After that my career flourished and I became a star of pornographic films. They're still about here and there – my wife doesn't know about them, of course . . .'

This tongue-in-cheek biography of Newman's appeared in *Playboy* magazine, June 1968, in an interview with Richard Warren Lewis. Of course, it was never intended that anyone should believe in these bizarre origins. With these fictions the evasive and self-effacing actor was making a joke against himself and his exceedingly normal, well-heeled and happy background with its lack of incident or trauma.

It was also a humorous attempt to provide a history acceptable to the expectations of the movie-going public who has always loved the tale of the boy or girl who makes good. There were many such in Hollywood – all those ordinary Joes or Jeans who had been poor and uneducated yet had had a dream. Against all odds they had gone on to make their mark in the glamorous world of showbiz, all those ex-lorry drivers, those daughters of sad, mad women

and wicked stepfathers, those strong, silent ex-penitentiary boys who finally had made it to fame and fortune. These were the favourite American tales but Newman, in real life, did not have one to tell. He, too, had worked hard, but rarely had to fight for opportunities. Invariably, these had found him first. During his early years, whenever things looked a little bit rough, something had always turned up in the nick of time and usually of a nature that suited him well. He was – and he is the first to admit it – always lucky. He considers himself the luckiest man in the world.

'Newman's luck' is a Hollywood cliché. And he was doubly lucky, of course. He possessed a talent that yielded fine fruits when opportunity came his way.

But this 'son of a miserable Indian' has never been able to understand why fate was so good to him, nor to feel that he deserved such fortune. Newman always harbours a fear that one day it may all disappear. 'I have a recurring nightmare,' he once said, 'in which I dream that the whole bottom is going to fall out of my career, that I will have paid several million dollars in taxes and will have no annuity to live on in my later years . . . Because acting comes so easily to me and because I've been fortunate enough to have made pictures that turned out O.K., it is very difficult for me to comprehend why the rewards should be so extraordinary. That's why I feel it might come to an abrupt end. And if it did, I would have to adjust to new circumstances. It isn't just the money, but the fact that I've become accustomed to a certain kind of living and recognition that may be totally destroyed. I worry so much that I'm lucky if I get five hours' sleep at night even between films . . .'

It is hard to imagine that Newman loses too many nights' sleep over the problem – he is prone to exaggeration when it comes to discussing his so-called failings – but clearly insecurity dogged him constantly. It was a healthy anxiety, however, and has prevented his ever becoming 'too big for his boots', an unattractive quality indigenous to his profession.

Hud, *1963*

Something else lies in that fabricated biography in *Playboy* which is more than just a joke, however. There has always been a part of Paul Newman that could have been the 'son of a poor invalid woman', who could have come from the wrong side of town. Even as a boy, behind that glowing exterior and gregarious charm another face existed. He was a dreamer and, in his own way, a loner. He had a secret self, unknown to others. He was enigmatic, but he could be what people wanted him to be. Without diminishing Newman's individuality, he was of a particular, though unusual, type – one that can be found in any walk of life.

The loner-dreamer invariably possesses a creative nature. Rebel-loners, with less ideal conditions of birth and opportunity than Newman's, have often had to turn their thwarted talents to less rewarding and productive ends. Had Newman been born into less privileged circumstances and had he not discovered acting, this vagabond drive could have festered until it grew into something intolerable in its lack of expression. By middle age it could have developed into neurosis, or had he been poor, perhaps to crime.

Newman is as far removed from such failed and crippled men as it is possible to imagine, yet he knows them and understands them. He could have become such a man and, behind the fiction of the boy who lost his father and virginity at fourteen, who provided for his poor family until he ran away to sea, then came back to make good, lies a degree of wish-fulfilment. The crazy biography in *Playboy* was a parody of his other self – his *alter ego*.

So far in his career this quality of Newman's had shone forth in his films only spasmodically. He now needed a part that would determine his unique film identity once and for all. The key lay – though no one was clearly aware of it at the time – in the full expression of his *alter ego*. Until now, despite his many successes, it was as though his career had been a road towards his final and proper destination. Soon, what this was would become clear.

As a natural extension of his affinity with loners, Newman had always been intrigued by a particularly American type. This was the kind of man who strives to the top unaided by others – the loner who makes good. Often this man is physically alluring, virile, attractive to both women and men, and has what it takes to become rich. Above all, he succeeds. At the same time, however, such a man runs the risk of losing his soul. His charisma and his charm tempt him to corruption. Newman understood the dangers of charm misused. He could have become just such a man, and he longed for the part that captured this.

After the recriminations which followed the release of *Exodus*, almost like magic everything fell into place. An opportunity presented itself which would settle any doubts about his career for all time. He was offered the role of Eddie Felson in a brilliant screenplay entitled *The Hustler*. 'I had a good feeling about this one right from the start,' says Newman.

The character of Eddie fitted Newman's abilities perfectly. His 'other' side found complete expression at last. In the legitimate medium of film he found the ideal means to release that part of himself, to purge some of the contradictions and baser elements of that *alter ego* from his system.

With Piper Laurie in The Hustler, *1961*

'Fast Eddie' was to be his best role yet. In the eyes of the world he strayed far from the traditional concept of a hero. Eddie, a skilled but devious pool player, makes his living by conning his opponents into thinking he is far less expert than is the truth. His ambition in life is to beat the country's top player, Minnesota Fats (an excellent performance by Jackie Gleason). Eddie is a glorious synthesis of all the loners and misfits Newman had played so well: Rocky, Ben Quick, Billy the Kid. Eddie is arrogant and mean, yet from somewhere deep within him a quality shines through. Inadequate in his ability to relate to others, Eddie's involvement with a sad, alcoholic quasi-hooker (played by Piper Laurie – another superb performance in the film) is a tentative but noble attempt at some kind of truthful communication. Their melancholy affair is doomed to failure, despite the love that develops between them. In the final, lethal battle with Fats, Eddie's ethical code is put to the test, together with his love for the girl. Corruption almost destroys him. He saves himself in the nick of time but at enormous cost. Newman brought off the performance to perfection.

When *The Hustler* was released, the reviews and acclaim for this film, directed by Robert Rossen, were, without exception, ecstatic. Paul V. Beckley summed up the view of all: 'The writing, the directing and the acting all have that kind of intense unanimity that convinces you everyone involved understood and felt what they were concerned with . . . Paul Newman has never looked more firmly

inside a role . . . ' Alton Cook of *Time* said of him: 'There is something extra this time in his intense ardour as the man who treats a game with religious zeal that at times amounts to mania. His standard is high but he has surpassed it this time.'

The film received nine Oscar nominations, including Newman's second as Best Actor. Incredibly he lost to Maximilian Schell, who won the coveted prize for a far less impressive performance in *Judgement at Nuremberg*. Newman did, however, win the British Academy Award for his role, and *The Hustler* has since become a screen classic.

The definitive image had been formed. Newman's magnetism now reached a worldwide audience who avidly awaited each new appearance. He represented the man that every male would like to have been and that every woman would like to have had. The image was perfectly suited to the times. It embodied the qualities that were currently most admired – instinctive intelligence unhampered by too much education, together with confidence, independence, the ability to hack it in life whatever the odds, toughness, sometimes meanness – all wrapped up with an irresistible charm.

Newman had acquired a considerable status within his profession. Apart from his talent and the sheer physical

With The Hustler *Newman's definitive image was formed – that of the tough, complicated loner*

power he generated on the screen, many of those who worked closely with him had come to admire him as an individual. He was recognized as a strong man who rejected the trappings of showbiz life. Both he and his wife were never afraid to voice their opinions. What had once been regarded as a lack of co-operation was now seen by many as virtue, in an age when old standards were under question. Newman is one of those beings rarely found in the movie world – a man with a mature and controlled personality. His private life was scandal-free, he enjoyed a happy marriage and had now become a father for the fifth time – Melissa, another daughter, had been born to Miss Woodward in 1961. He was intelligent, civilized, but not a man to cross swords with. As an actor with a stable, modest, yet powerful personality he shared the same kind of integrity that had been respected in the late Humphrey Bogart.

Perhaps basking a little in the triumph of *The Hustler* Newman's next film was chosen for reasons other than its intellectual merit. In *Paris Blues*, a lightweight and rather poor film, he appeared as a jazz musician. He had been lured into doing it by the prospect of working with his wife and old friends. Also, the Newmans loved Europe, another motive for doing the film, which was to be shot in Paris. A long-time friend, Martin Ritt, was director and the musical score was superlative. Louis Armstrong played music composed by Duke Ellington. There were many friends in Paris and making the film was, at least, good fun. In fact the only thing wrong with it was its script. Too many writers had been employed and too many changes made.

When the film finally opened this imbalance showed only too clearly, although the Newmans themselves worked well together. *Variety* criticized 'the screenplay's failure to bring any true identity to any of these four characters. As a result, their relationships are vague and superficial. Furthermore, except for sporadic interludes, none of the four players can achieve clarity, arouse sympathy, or sustain concern. This is especially disappointing in view of the acknowledged calibre of performers such as Newman, Poitier and Miss Woodward.'

Never make a film just for fun, Newman learned. As always, he tried to make the best of, and to learn from, bad experiences. At least he had met and worked with Sidney Poitier and the seeds of an important friendship had been sown.

The unenthusiastic reception for *Paris Blues* did nothing to affect the projects offered to the Newmans when they returned to America. They were more sought after than ever. But in spite of his successes Newman was still not a wealthy man. While he was now able to pick and choose his parts, he had so far been unable to avoid the tyranny of the studio system and its religion of expedience and greed.

Now, in an attempt to achieve some financial independence, he formed a corporation with director Martin Ritt. Short-lived though it was, the partnership produced a couple of notable films and was important in being the first decisive step Newman took towards being in business for himself.

After *Paris Blues*, Newman needed a role to sustain the image he had so successfully acquired with *The Hustler*. Fortunately, his performance in that movie had been so strong that his latest failure passed almost unnoticed. It was

only a matter of time before another challenging and powerful role presented itself to him. He was offered the part of Chance Wayne in the film version of Tennessee Williams's *Sweet Bird of Youth*. Having already played the role on Broadway, Newman was intimate with the part. His command is clearly demonstrated in the finished product. He is perfect as the confident opportunist whose skill lies in his sexual seduction of women. At the same time, Wayne is a dreamer and, deep down, insecure. When he falls in love he becomes confused and childlike. Newman played opposite his friend Geraldine Page as Alexandra and a touching newcomer, Shirley Knight, as Heavenly. The film was a big success, despite criticisms of Hollywood's compulsion to water down a strong story.

Feeling more confident than ever, Newman next appeared in *Adventures of a Young Man*, based on Hemingway's story of the same title. His was a small, cameo role, but Newman was now secure enough to break with Hollywood tradition and saw nothing demeaning in a small role which he liked and had played before in television – that of 'the battler'. Also, the film was directed by his associate Martin Ritt. Playing the old and punch-drunk fighter, Newman was almost unrecognizable behind his elaborate and unflattering make-up. His performance, however, was excellent. He saw working in this off-beat, interesting film as a real challenge to his acting abilities, and this was what he considered his craft should be.

Deriving both pleasure and profit from their partnership, Newman's next venture was again with Martin Ritt. This film was to become almost as celebrated as *The Hustler*. Newman played the character of the title, *Hud*, an embittered cattleman, ambitious and selfish. It was another of those gem roles, suited to his uncanny understanding of such men, which are scattered like diamonds throughout his sometimes experimental career. Before filming, Newman, as always, spent time in Texas getting the feel of the man and his surroundings. He worked on a cattle ranch, insisting upon learning to do the job properly and refusing to be treated differently from the other ranchers. By the time filming had begun, Newman even walked like a rancher and his hands had become coarsened and calloused from the continual handling of rope. He *was* the part.

Hud was released to ecstatically enthusiastic reviews. Bosley Crowther in the *New York Times* wrote: 'While it looks a modern western and is an outdoor drama indeed, *Hud* is as wide and profound a contemplation of the human condition as one of the plays of Eugene O'Neill. The strikingly important thing about it is the clarity with which it unreels. The sureness and integrity of it are as crystal clear as the plot is spare . . . with a fine cast of performers he [Martin Ritt] has people who behave and talk so truly that it is hard to shake them out of your mind. Paul Newman is tremendous – a potent, voracious man, restless with all his crude ambitions, arrogant with his contempt and churned up inside with all the meanness and misgivings of himself.'

Praise indeed. *Hud* was more critically acclaimed than any other Newman film. A huge commercial success, it received no less than seven Oscar nominations. Newman obtained his third Oscar nomination for Best Actor. Patricia Neal, for

Newman the clown. At the party after the opening of Baby Want a Kiss

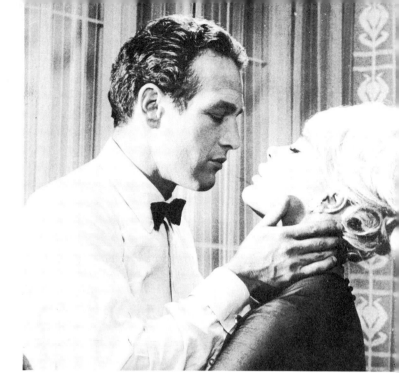

Right: The Prize *with Elke Sommer, 1963*

Below and left: Newman finds himself at a nudist convention in a scene from The Prize

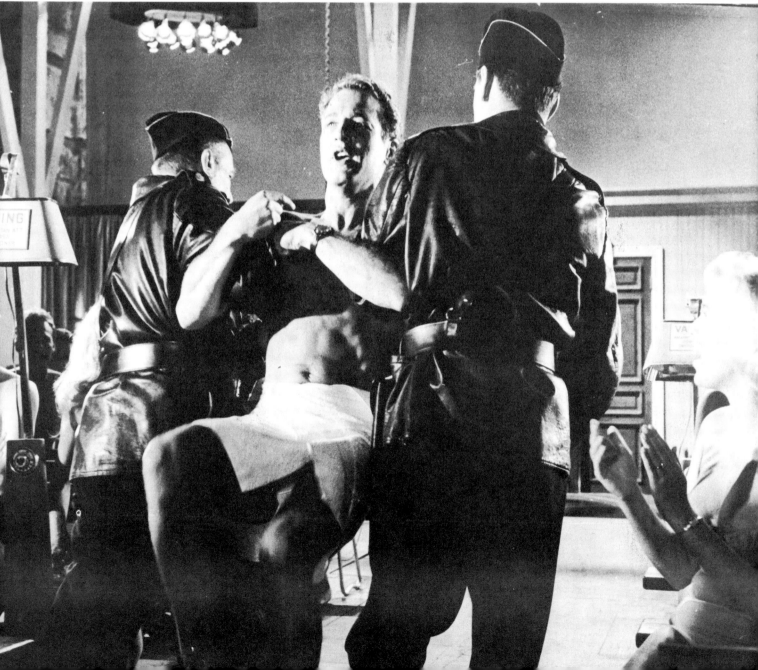

her magically lethargic yet sharp performance, received the Best Actress Award. (It is interesting to note that in many of Newman's best films there is a stunning female counterpart portrayal – Piper Laurie's in *The Hustler*, and Shirley Knight's in *Sweet Bird of Youth*, among others.) In an era when people spoke of the decline of the big-star system in Hollywood, *Hud* was a clear confirmation that strong, individualistic actors could still attract huge audiences and make money.

Hud brought Newman real freedom. He could now allocate his time as he wished to scripts and projects of his choice. Oddly, now that he had finally achieved it, Newman seemed for a while uncomfortable with this new liberty. It was as though the years of compliance to others had blunted his judgement. The next group of films, all from scripts he had chosen himself, show an almost wilful determination to play indifferent roles. At the same time this period was clearly an attempt to extend himself, to expand his horizons, to escape from the highly successful but, to an actor of Newman's ambitions, limited confines of his 'loner' roles. Relentlessly, he attempted to master the art of comedy. Trying to develop from his brilliant portrayals of irresponsible men, he attempted the thriller genre, playing worldly-wise detectives, spies and the 'a man's gotta do what a man's gotta do' parts that had always abounded in Hollywood. Occasionally these did work – and very well indeed – proving Newman to be an actor who *could* diversify his talents. But the 'wrong' parts can be seen as the one serious flaw in Newman's long and fruitful career. He wanted to prove himself master of all. The next half-dozen films following *Hud* in 1963 were competent but mediocre.

The first of those mostly forgettable films was the comedy *A New Kind of Love*, in which he once more played opposite Miss Woodward. Again, the film was set in Paris. It was a silly film and once again the critics drew attention to Newman's lack of ease in comedy. The movie was panned. Judith Christ in the *New York Herald Tribune* summed up: 'The pow-bam-sock-wow subtle sophistication of the jazzed-up now-its-black-and-white-now-its-Technicolour introduction, all to the tune of a Sinatra song, provides immediate stupefaction and sets the tone for the ensuing banalities, commercial juvenile sex play and sophomoric camera tricks that go on for nigh two unsolid hours.'

Newman's final film of 1963, *The Prize*, did not fare much better. The picture was a mindless romantic adventure story in which a womanizing Nobel Prize novelist (Newman) sets out to solve the kidnapping of a colleague. Attempting to hold its audience in their seats by suspense, the film also tried to play for laughs, an uneasy combination at the best of times. The film was received without enthusiasm.

The first half of 1964 brought Newman's next comedy, *What a Way to Go*, in which Shirley MacLaine was his co-star. An improvement was noted by a few critics in Newman's facility for comedy but, in general, the film was not praised.

During the same year the Newmans played together again – this time in an off-Broadway production of the James Costigan comedy, *Baby Want a Kiss*. It was a well-constructed and funny play and Newman proved that he *could* indeed play comedy – if the part was suited to him, as it was in this case. John Chapman in the *New York Daily News* observed: 'The players, Paul Newman and Joanne Woodward . . . are admirable, stylish comedians, and they have time and room in which to exercise their undoubted gifts.'

In his next movie, Newman once more teamed up with his old friend Martin Ritt. *The Outrage*, based on the Japanese film *Rashomon*, remains one of Newman's favourite films. The critics, however, were less enthusiastic. While they appreciated his earnest and often successful attempt at in-depth characterization of a completely new kind of role they regarded the film as gimmicky and over the top. Judith Crist observed in the *New York Herald Tribune*: 'Perhaps *Rashomon* cannot stand the transition from East to West or to modern times. As it is, *The Outrage* emerges as a sententious theme with dull variations . . .'

Newman persisted in this compulsion to take on roles outside his range. In his next film, *Lady L*, in which he starred opposite Sophia Loren, he was judged competent in a banal role but little more.

Then, again, a stroke of luck occurred. The mediocre *Lady L*. was held back from release for several months and in the meantime Newman was offered a fine role and a worthwhile film. He needed both badly. The role of Harper, in *The Moving Target*, was an anti-hero characterization of the kind he could be relied upon to play well. The rest of the cast was superb and included Lauren Bacall, Janet Leigh, Julie Harris and Shelley Winters. It was a tight, entertaining thriller with, this time, a wholly successful blend of real suspense and wry humour.

His luck was in again. *The Moving Target* recovered for Newman all his lost ground and more. It brought him to the brink of superstardom and was a huge box office hit. The *Saturday Review* was typical in its praise: 'Newman, as the hard, sardonic shamus, works with the same skill and consistency that marked his performances in *Hud* and *The Hustler*.'

His next two films, *Torn Curtain* in 1966 and *Hombre* in 1967, received mixed reactions. In *Torn Curtain* it was clear that the separate artistry of Hitchcock and Newman did not blend well together. In *Hombre*, Newman received either faint praise – 'Paul Newman leads a uniformly competent cast' (*Variety*) – or frank dismissal - 'Mr Newman plays his *Hombre* with dour one-note grimness, hardly changing any expression on his face' (Leo Mistikin, *New York Morning Telegraph*).

And then, as has happened time and again throughout Newman's career, he leaped back into spectacular form. In the latter half of 1967 he was perfectly cast in the hard-hitting *Cool Hand Luke*. In this sombre, intelligent movie he played the part of an individualistic convict on a chain gang who gains the respect of his fellows and who eventually dies – the price for being true to himself.

The film won Newman his fourth Academy Award nomination and it was considered a serious injustice that he did not receive the Oscar. The critics' acclaim verged on the worshipful. Newman's brillant perception, vitality and skill were recognized as unique.

He was now forty-two years old. He had found his genre and his place in the sun. His less inspiring 'experiments' were forgiven, so admired was his acting at its best. But Newman was stubborn. Even after the phenomenal success of *Cool*

Flying high with Sophia Loren in Lady L, *1965*

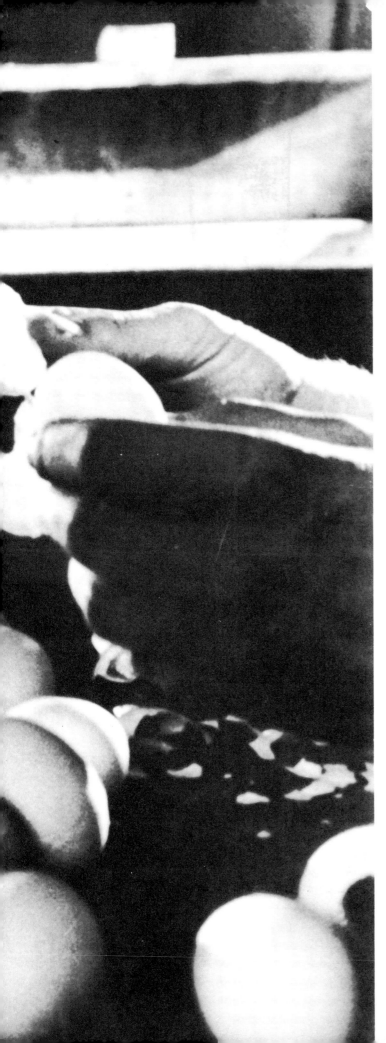

Hand Luke he plunged into yet another insubstantial comedy, *The Secret War of Harry Frigg*, which received faint praise and the familiar comments that the excellent Mr Newman should keep away from farce.

He was still determined to experiment, to extend himself. In the past, such experimentation had not led to a mastery of fresh areas of his craft, yet he was still burning with ambition to branch out, to find something which would extend his talent to the limit.

He looked to his wife, who encouraged him to take chances. The forties are a rough passage for many men, who for the first time face the fact that time is not endless and confront their own mortality. Newman was no exception to the restlessness of that watershed decade.

By now the couple had three daughters, for Claire had been born in 1965. Miss Woodward herself, while still a devoted mother, was hungry for something more challenging.

Scripts and ideas were constantly proposed to both of them. One day a modest but truthful tale was given to Miss Woodward. After reading it she passed it to her husband for his views. And a new direction suddenly became clear . . .

Left: Cool Hand Luke, *1967*

Following pages: Dominating the P.O.W. commandant (Werner Peters) in The Secret War of Harry Frigg, *1968*

7
A MARRIAGE OF TRUE MINDS

Paul Newman's career had begun with disaster. *The Silver Chalice* was a crass débâcle, an artistic and financial flop, its new star acknowledged only as stripping well, a handsome meatball who came on with the pretentious mannerisms of a third-rate Brando.

Yet through luck, determination and, above all, talent, Newman overcame this inauspicious start to become one of the world's leading film actors. It is nothing short of astonishing that he has not yet received an Oscar for the half-dozen performances he has transformed into classics. He has, of course, received many nominations – multiple honours in themselves – and acquired enough tokens of success to satisfy most men. In 1966 he was named the World's Favourite Actor at the 33rd Annual Golden Globes Banquet. A year later he was nominated Best Actor of the Year by the National Association of Theatre Owners.

By 1968 he had become a doyen of the exclusive Hollywood establishment. The privileged few who reached these heights – players such as Humphrey Bogart, Gary Cooper, Kirk Douglas, John Wayne and, later, Robert Redford and Steve McQueen – graduate from the common fraternity of Hollywood. Liberated talents, they soar free and answer to no one but themselves, for of their audiences they are assured. They have succeeded despite the system, not because of it. When, as with Newman, their judgement errs, their mistakes are overlooked. Provided these are not too often or too defiantly repeated, in the world's eyes they can do no wrong. They have become superstars. They live in a state of grace.

The problem was that this rare standing, this breathless adulation and mass renown, was not a condition that Newman had either desired or striven for. What he had achieved in terms of status was irrelevant to him. He wanted challenge, or more; something else.

In contrast to her husband, Joanne Woodward, in her first major role, had begun her movie career with a massive success. After two small, unnoticed parts, her leading role in *The Three Faces of Eve* won her the Academy Award for Best Actress. Her film career started at the very top. Paradoxically, this had been a disadvantage. How do you follow that?

An unusual actress by Hollywood standards, she was at her best in intelligent, complex roles, and such female parts were, and are, not numerous. Apart from the brillance of her début, Miss Woodward had been unusually fortunate in her first major film. Although *The Three Faces of Eve* was a seriously flawed film, Miss Woodward's role provided a rare platform for her special skills. Playing three separate women who are one requires subtle understanding of the almost imperceptible but vital nuances which link the characters. It was an intricate part and only an exceptionally astute and instinctive actress could have made it a success. The role was a showcase for Joanne Woodward's talents.

Suitable parts to match those gifts, however, had since proved rare. Although Miss Woodward appeared in some good films and played well, these were not commercially successful and did little to extend her reputation. *The Fugitive Kind* and *A Fine Madness* are typical of such pictures, ventures in advance of their times.

The truth was that Hollywood undervalued one of its most exciting actresses. Miss Woodward was offered roles almost always of a Southern drop-out or a neurotic. Aware, alert, gifted with a clear understanding of her herself, she yearned to extend herself. She had *done* all that. But she was never given the opportunities she deserved. Fortunately, she was happy in her private life and, up to a point, was able to sublimate her frustrations in bringing up three lively girls with the support of a man she adored and who shared with her his thriving career. Newman was always her champion. Her role as a wife and mother failed to blunt his esteem of her talents. Miss Woodward was too clever to be totally satisfied by this role however. A generous woman, she never deprived her children of herself, but there was a certain animosity towards the details of that life, the domestic preoccupations, P.T.A. meetings and living through the young. She was always searching for new creative outlets and never gave up trying to discover where these might lie.

With Joanne at the New York Film Critics' Awards, 1968

One day, a writer friend called Stuart Stern gave Joanne Woodward a book to read. Entitled *The Jest of God* and written by Margaret Laurence, the heroine of the story was a self-effacing Connecticut school teacher who, at the age of thirty-five, panics at the remorseless passage of her days. The character, along with the others in the tale, leads a humdrum, ordinary existence but becomes desperate to make some mark in life, however small. She decides actively to search for the happening that will change her and, mistakenly, transfers this hunger into a frantic hunt for love. Unworldly, inexperienced, she confuses sex with love and suffers the consequences in disillusion.

It was a quiet, delicate and touching story and Miss Woodward loved it. She understood and empathized deeply with the heroine. She persuaded her husband to read the book. At first Newman was not so enthusiastic as his wife, but her excitement and determination proved contagious and soon he became caught up in the activity that would ultimately bring *The Jest of God* to the screen.

The problem was finding finance. Even with Miss Woodward's name attached, the project was hardly Hollywood's idea of entertainment. The money men considered it, at best, a small budget movie with limited appeal. But by now the Newmans were both committed to the idea and undeterred by repeated failures to secure backing. Soon Newman found himself agreeing to act as producer to keep the whole venture afloat.

Meanwhile, Stuart Stern, who had written the screenplay of an early Newman film, *The Rack*, and also the script for *Rebel Without a Cause*, started work on *The Jest of God*. He, too, was in love with the story. Time passed, but the Newmans, together with Stern, failed to find the necessary finance.

Newman was giving much thought to his future during this period. He had considered the idea of directing, but lacked the confidence to put himself to the test. Yet he knew he could, for as early on as 1958 he had directed and produced a television short, *On the Harmfulness of Tobacco*, based on Anton Chekhov's play of the same title.

Now, with an idea but no funds, his directing début was thrust upon him. He was obliged to take the chance. This was not a difficult decision. Newman had become so involved with the project and so tuned into the actress who would play the lead – his wife – that his next move can be seen as inevitable.

Newman, naturally enough, did not inspire particular confidence, since this was his first venture as a director. His name as a star, however, elevated the status of his project and it was taken a little more seriously. Finally Warner Brothers came up with $700,000 – not much, even for a small budget movie, but enough for the team to start production.

Excitement fired them. By hook or by crook the picture would be made – but not without difficulty. To produce the film in a Hollywood studio would cost in the region of $2½ million. Their budget was a third of this. Stringent economies would be necessary and the goodwill of all involved was crucial.

A vast saving was made possible by reason of the Newmans' own unshakable commitment. They worked for

With Joanne at the première party for Cool Hand Luke, *1967*

nothing, taking a percentage in the (speculative) profits in lieu of fee. Their enthusiasm was infectious and others chose to become involved in the same fashion.

Newman took pains to obtain the best talent and technicians available. Dédé Allen, one of the industry's best film cutters, agreed to edit, and stood beside Newman from the first day of shooting. Stuart Stern, the script writer, also remained on the set throughout production.

Newman was lucky in that he was surrounded by creative, first-rate talents who believed in his ideas and supported him in his début. The sensitive, almost perfect, finished product was an indication of how much could be achieved by such unorthodox yet dedicated co-operation.

Further costs were saved by compressing the shooting schedule into only five weeks. The vast expense involved in making the film in Hollywood was avoided by converting an old gymnasium in Danbury, Connecticut, into a makeshift studio. Any disadvantages caused by lack of facilities were compensated for by the authenticity of locations and the use, in small parts, of ordinary people from the local community. Newman extracted some marvellous vignette performances from these non-actors, a true sign of directing skill. The film crew, who usually prefer to remain cynically distanced from their employers and artists, also became personally involved in the desire for excellence and success. Morale, for all the inconvenience, was very high, and the experience immensely satisfying for all concerned.

Newman, more than anyone, was delighted by the experience and the outcome of this, his first foray into feature direction. Despite technical inexperience, a shortcoming noticed particularly by the camera crew, he proved a sensitive and skilled handler of both story and people. He inspired affection and respect from both the professionals and the locals who appeared in the film. In other circumstances sometimes aloof and taciturn, Newman managed to create an atmosphere of total rapport between all those involved in the production.

He spoke of his aspiration to direct to journalist Jane Wilson during the filming: 'I'm curious about my taste, my dramatic selection, my technical ability with the camera. There's no way to find out but to get up there and do it, and then let the people hit you with baseball bats. I've always wanted to direct because I've always enjoyed most the peripheral things about acting, the rehearsals and the field trips, the exploration of character and the whole intellectual exercise of the thing. I enjoy this more than actually getting up on stage or in front of a camera.'

Working together in this new relationship was a joy for the director and his wife. Newman's understanding and appreciation of Miss Woodward's gift, the fact that he knew her so well, combined with their shared view on how this simple story should be told, resulted in the best performance of the actress's career. There was total understanding between them, a secret language of communication.

Two oft-quoted remarks sum up the satisfaction both experienced in this first partnership. Newman said, 'My wife Joanne is in it. She is brilliant. God, she's marvellous. We have the same acting vocabulary, and that made it a hell of a lot easier – I just gave her one-line zingers like "pinch it" or "thicken it" and she knew what I meant. I can't think of any other actress that the experience of directing could have been better with.' Woodward said simply, 'With due respect to some of the film directors I've worked with, I just wish

Paul could direct every movie I'll ever make.' They discovered a completely new dimension to their relationship, already so good. They could give to each other creatively; each was able to bring out the best within the other.

The film came out in 1968 under the title of *Rachel, Rachel*. Bemused, Warners found a totally unexpected hit on its hands. From conception right through production no other film had attracted more scepticism and less enthusiasm. The story was a *downer*, for God's sake. Only upon screening did it become clear that this downer contained a magic which reached straight to the heart of a mass audience.

At the time, Newman spoke of the film's aims, 'It singles out the unspectacular heroism of the sort of person you wouldn't even notice if you passed them on the street. The steps the characters take are really the steps that humanity takes – not the Churchills, not the Roosevelts, not the Napoleons, but the little people who cast no shadow and leave no footprints. Maybe it can encourage the people who see it to take those little steps in life that can lead to something bigger. Maybe they won't, but the point of the movie is that you've got to take the steps, regardless of the consequences.'

Newman has always been a humane man, but as an actor he had rarely had the opportunity to reveal this side of his nature – he plays best as his *alter ego*. As a director, however, he showed himself as one who understands the poignancy of human waste. Living in a world where such sensitivity can become blunted, it is a credit to Newman that his sense of compassion should remain so sharp.

The film was a triumph from every point of view. The critics raved over the achievement and the director was lauded for this auspicious début. At the same time, Miss Woodward was hailed as America's finest natural actress.

Richard Schickel in *Life* magazine summed up the overall reaction: 'The film was clearly undertaken in a spirit too rare in American life. That is to say, a star, Joanne Woodward, and a screen writer, Stuart Stern, discovered a novel, Margaret Laurence's *The Jest of God*, that was, to them, something more than a mere property. Instead, it was a difficult and delicate thing that challenged them as artists, something they felt they simply had to make. They apparently encountered enormous difficulties in obtaining the relatively modest backing they required, and it was not until Miss Woodward's husband, Paul Newman, put his plentiful clout behind the project by agreeing to direct it that they could go ahead. Everyone involved thereupon did his work with taste, conviction, and solid, sometimes brillant, craftsmanship. Stern's script, despite a tendency to tell rather than show, rings with gentle irony and rueful truth. Miss Woodward demonstrates again that she is perhaps the only female star of our day capable of genuine naturalism, submerging self and image in a subtle, disciplined performance that avoids showiness, excessive sentiment, self-consciousness. As a director, Newman is anything but the bouncing boy we are accustomed to seeing on our screens. He has a sensitive, slightly melancholic eye for something most American movies miss – the texture of

Eli Wallach's birthday party at the Waltz of the Toreador *opening*

ordinary life. He displays, moreover, a feel for emotional nuances and a technical sureness; he is neither too radical nor too conservative. That is remarkable in a first film.'

Rachel, Rachel, commercially successful, was nominated for several Oscars as the Academy Awards. These included Best Picture, Best Actress, Best Supporting Actress (Estelle Parsons) and Best Screenplay. Newman won the New York Film Critics' Award for 1968 as Best Director. Joanne was voted Best Actress.

The film was the most important achievement of the Newmans' lives to date. Through it, Miss Woodward was rescued from the doldrums of her career. For Newman, it brought recognition, status and esteem in his newly-chosen directing role, at forty-plus a new start. A new dimension also to a marriage that had lasted over ten years and produced three children, a deepening enrichment to their partnership.

In its especial way *Rachel, Rachel* was the Newmans' gift to one another.

Now Newman was besieged with offers to direct. But, under no pressure, he could afford to wait for a truly worthwhile project.

Making *Rachel, Rachel* inspired him to consider alternatives to the big money, big names, big story requirement that formed the traditional Hollywood method. He could produce good films at half the cost and still make a profit. He had proved so. In June 1969 Newman formed a corporation with his old friend from *Paris Blues* Sidney Poitier, and Barbra Streisand. Later joined by Steve McQueen in 1971, they named it First Artists Production Company. The idea was to appear in productions which they themselves would finance and distribute. Newman described the aims of the company at the time: 'The motion picture industry can and must be streamlined. For too long we have lived with outdated production and distribution. The purpose of this company, among other things, will not necessarily be to economize, but to put production on a more efficient basis. The money belongs on the screen.'

As an actor, Newman was now receiving a million dollars plus for a picture. He found himself spending more and more time on financial detail and in endless discussions of profit percentage. He resented the drain on his creative energy such activity involved. Although it would be a couple of years before First Artists would release their first picture, the forming of the company was a brave attempt at breaking with convention, and easing such pressures, to get down to the basics of the business – making films.

Newman had also formed a company with his wife and with director John Foreman called the Newman/Foreman Company, and Newman's next movie, *Winning*, was the first produced under this banner. Universal Studios had commissioned the script of this lavish $7 million production with the Newmans in mind as the leading players. *Winning* was a racing drama, its climax the contest between two racing drivers (Newman and Robert Wagner) in the Indianapolis 500-mile race. What might at first appear to be an exploitation epic was, in fact, a serious and suspenseful film interlaced with human drama. Both Newmans liked the

Newman, Streisand and Poitier incorporating First Artists Production Company, 1969

script and wanted to work together. Furthermore, for some years now Newman had been developing a growing passion for cars and racing. He was already driving racing cars as a hobby and *Winning* seemed an enjoyable way to spend the next few months.

In fact, making this film about the racing world motivated Newman's late entry into real racing, the passion later becoming so strong it almost became a third career. For *Winning* he was obliged to extend his driving skills, and he spent time before filming at the Bob Bondurant School of High Performance Driving in Santa Ana, California. He discovered a real and instinctive facility for the sport.

Spectacular footage was incorporated into the movie of the seventeen-car crash which occurred in the 1968 Indianapolis race. Refusing a double for the dangerous matching scenes Newman was insured for $3 million.

The story was of a top driver, Frank Capua (Newman) who falls in love with and marries Elora (Joanne Woodward), the mother of a teenage boy. However, Frank's obsession with racing takes him from home, and his neglected wife has an affair with his main opponent in the race. To add to Frank's humiliation, his wife's lover is offered the car he had set his heart on for the big race. The teenage son, sympathetic with his stepfather, restores Frank's morale and he rebuilds his own car. Tested to the limit, he wins the race and, realizing the cost to himself and others of his folly, goes after Elora for a reconciliation.

Reviews were good. *Variety* reported: 'Newman underplays his part throughout, resulting in one of his better performances. He is ideally cast as the racer, and those sequences in which he is racing are convincingly portrayed.' Howard Thompson in the *New York Times* wrote: 'Probably the best-rounded and most appealing personalized film of this kind ever made . . . The Newmans are both splendid.'

Within weeks of its release the picture had proved itself a success at the box office and eventually returned huge profits on its considerable investment. Its success was neatly timed – particularly so, in that it was actually released before the prestigious *Rachel, Rachel*. Critical acclaim for Newman as director was still ahead.

For both the Newmans the future looked bright.

Left: Victor (at the age of fifty-seven) in the Kendall Cup Nationals at Lime Rock Park, 1982

Following pages: Taking it easy at the top. Joanne and Newman in 1969

8
SUPERSTAR

It's a wet spring morning in Chicago. The morning rush has died down at Union Station, but today routines are in disarray. Today there is something in the air. The predictability of countless other Mondays have been shattered. There is an electric expectancy which all who pass through can sense around them.

The clue to this change in atmosphere lies in the astonishing sight that greets the eye in and around the vast, high-ceilinged waiting room. More than 1,000 people wait restlessly behind police cordons. Most of them are women. It seems none has a train to catch, although many who have just stepped off one become mesmerized and stay to join the throng.

The crowd presses against the barriers. The police are here in force, as are the press and television news crews. 'What's going on?' asks a newcomer, 'Was there an accident?' The crowd just wait, most in silence.

In fact, Union Station is being used for a location sequence in the forthcoming movie, *The Sting*, and the crowd are patiently awaiting a glimpse of its stars.

Meanwhile, director George Roy Hill is rehearsing the scene with camera crew, stand-in and extras. Fascinated, the crowd watch this work, so exciting, so different from their own occupations. There is a lively tension in the atmosphere, although the onlookers are orderly and conduct their occasional conversations in whispers. They are in awe. Suddenly, a high-pitched squeal cracks the murmurous spell. 'Oh my *God*, look!! Jesus Christ, it's *him*! It's Paul Newman!'

Newman, followed by Robert Redford and Robert Shaw, walks slowly down the centre aisle of the vast room. He is wearing a three-piece suit and a fedora, his costume for the picture. At five foot nine he is shorter and slighter than expected – on film he seems a big man – but in no way does this diminish his magnetism. The eyes seem lit from within and the crowd falls silent as he passes by.

Redford, similarly attired, defers to Newman's seniority. He has his share of admirers among the throng but is a relative newcomer to the Big League.

Shaw's costume is a camel-hair overcoat and black homburg. Few here are familiar with this brilliant British actor, but he too radiates an awe-inspiring presence. The trio seem to have stepped from another time and place, and their stylish attire only adds to the mystique that surrounds the scene.

For a brief moment Newman's blue eyes are raised to survey his public, who gaze back, silent. Then he grins and the smile spreads across his features, lighting up his whole face. It is irresistible and the audience break out with a spontaneous roar. They cheer, they applaud, they whoop their appreciation. It is like the first night of a Broadway hit or the response to a politician's speech. Newman, however, seems embarrassed by the response he has aroused and, after raising his hands in parody of a champ, he hurries off to work.

In an hour it's all over. As the crew pack up and make ready to leave, a young broker from the Commodities Exchange, which lies next door to Union, introduces himself to Newman with an offer to show him around the Mid-Western's Stock Exchange. Surprisingly, he agrees. He's genuinely interested, finance and commodities were part of his college studies. Redford, Shaw and director Hill decide to go along.

As they pass through the interlinking departments of the Exchange, Newman acquires an entourage of hundreds. People want to touch him. Men shake his hand. Women pluck at his sleeve. They all want to feel that he is real.

The most dramatic result of Newman's presence, however, is that work comes to a complete standstill in the normally frenetic Exchange. Nobody is trading. Nobody answers the phones.

And no one gets an autograph, though Newman is polite in his refusals. He has long since given up signing his name. The more confident employees desperately want to talk to him. Even the president of the Commodities Exchange has to shake his hand. It's been impossible to view the natural function of the Exchange. It takes some time for work to start again when Newman finally leaves.

That fine actor, the late Robert Shaw, was with Newman during the whole of that April day. In an interview in *Rolling Stone* he commented on Newman's popularity as he witnessed it then: 'There's no question about it – that was a pretty powerful reaction . . . I found it absolutely *amazing* that those businessmen should stop their transactions – I presume they dropped thousands of dollars in trade –

'. . . There's something photogenic – a chemistry. What the hell is it? . . . But he certainly has it . . .' (Robert Shaw)

simply because of Newman's presence . . . it's the same reaction as if any fairy-tale princess comes to town . . . obviously he carries for them enormous glamour . . . he absolutely has a quality which is remarkable on the screen . . . something that hasn't particularly to do with him as a person or anything else . . . what I mean is, you cannot define this kind of magnetism that he has any more than you can define a kind of animal magnetism that Olivier has, or one or two others. But he has it . . . it's a quality that's so powerful that I don't know where it came from. A lot of very good actors don't have it at all . . . There's something photogenic – a chemistry. What the hell is it? I don't know, but he certainly has it. If Newman were a completely unknown actor and had two lines in a pot-boiler he would absolutely stand out . . . Olivier's the same. Burton's the same . . . They all have this elusive quality that you cannot nail down.'

As for the owner of these magical qualities himself, he displayed characteristic modesty in response to the near worship his presence now evoked. His reaction to the day's events was as follows: 'I'm always just faintly embarrassed by all this, if that makes any sense. I mean, yesterday we apparently stopped the market. It's like sticking a gun in your mouth. I had no idea it was going to be like that. *Whew*!'

For several years before *The Sting* Newman was a famous movie star accustomed to the loss of freedom and privacy that accompany such success. Wherever he went in public he attracted a small crowd and had become skilled in dealing with awe-struck fans and deflecting the advances from women of every age and shape.

But that mob scene in Chicago was something else, beyond anything he had previously encountered. In *The Sting* he made the quantum leap from star to superstar. Yet Newman had attained the height of his career before he became a superstar. The 'superstar' films themselves, while being unusual, highly entertaining cult films, were not his most creatively interesting. They did not attract his best reviews, but nothing could detract from their astonishing, hysterical reception. Both the pictures in which he appeared as 'superstar' hit a nerve in audiences all over the world.

The acquisition of superstar status began unexpectedly. Delighted by reactions to *Winning*, and, even more so, *Rachel, Rachel*, Newman had been in no hurry to decide on his next picture.

The script of *Butch Cassidy and the Sundance Kid* had been circulating in Hollywood for some time before it caught Newman's attention. It was thought of as no big deal, a kooky Western, a light, half-true adventure story about a bunch of cowboys. But Newman saw potential in the story. He liked the relationship between Butch, the gang leader, and his partner, Sundance. When he revealed his liking for the script, suddenly the movie industry became extremely interested in the project. When it was learned that yet another prestigious star, Steve McQueen, was also keen on playing in the picture, *Butch Cassidy and the Sundance Kid* became the most desirable property in Hollywood. Fortunately, by this time the Newman/Foreman Company had managed to acquire the option.

With Newman cast as Butch, the role of the Sundance Kid was given to Robert Redford, and the part of the girl to Katherine Ross. George Roy Hill was director and Burt Bacharach and Hal David produced the music and title song, 'Raindrops Keep Falling on my Head', which would add to the film's success by becoming a huge hit.

During filming a spontaneous affection quickly developed between Newman and Redford and a friendship formed between the two, who shared much in common. Both understood the pressures of stardom, both valued privacy, both enjoyed long-lasting and successful marriages, both were hypersensitive about being valued on mere looks, both were involved in the ecological movement and both were regarded as maddeningly elusive by journalists the world over. In the completed film there is a sense of brotherly comradeship between the two. Newman says, 'You know, I don't think people realize what that picture was all about. It's a love affair between two men. The girl is incidental.'

But Newman underestimates his audiences. While they may not have considered the film a 'love affair between two men', there is no doubt that the warm relationship between Butch and Sundance gives the movie its particular appeal. The feelings in the film are expressed between the men, and the girl is a device for them to interact with each other, to the extent that they almost share her.

The story was loosely based on two outlaws who thrived for a while in the early 1900s. Newman at last found himself in a role which allowed him to demonstrate successfully the mellow, underplayed humour that had failed so disastrously in previous films. In a character who was human, poignant, and a little bit crazy, comedy became a different, more subtle instrument in Newman's hands.

The picture's ultimate triumph took all those involved by surprise. While it is certainly one of the most endearing films of all time, *Butch Cassidy* was, in many ways, an insubstantial movie. Yet reviews for its two stars, Newman and Redford, and its director, George Roy Hill, were extravagant in their praise. Judith Christ of the *New York Times*, often a harsh critic, wrote: 'In the hands of Newman and Redford . . . Goldman [the writer] and Hill . . . it's a glorious game, an affectionate one – and one made meaningful.'

The public took the film to their hearts. Something inexplicable and magical took place on screen. A cult was born and Newman became a superstar, a legend. His partner, Redford, established though unemployed and broke before the movie, enjoyed a similar fate. He won the British Academy Award for Best Actor while Katherine Ross, who had not gone unnoticed in her challenging role, received the Academy's Best Actress Award. Newman, who had waited some fifteen years now for the Oscar that he so obviously deserved, once more was denied this honour. His reward was to become Number One World Box Office Star. The picture grossed over $30 million and was to prove the biggest money-making Western in the history of motion pictures.

The world, it seemed, was at Newman's feet. The Number One Superstar, however, did not allow this exalted status to change either his lifestyle or the beliefs he had always held.

Compromising with Joanne. At the American Ballet Theatre Gala, 1975
Following page: Butch Cassidy and the Sundance Kid, *1970*

86

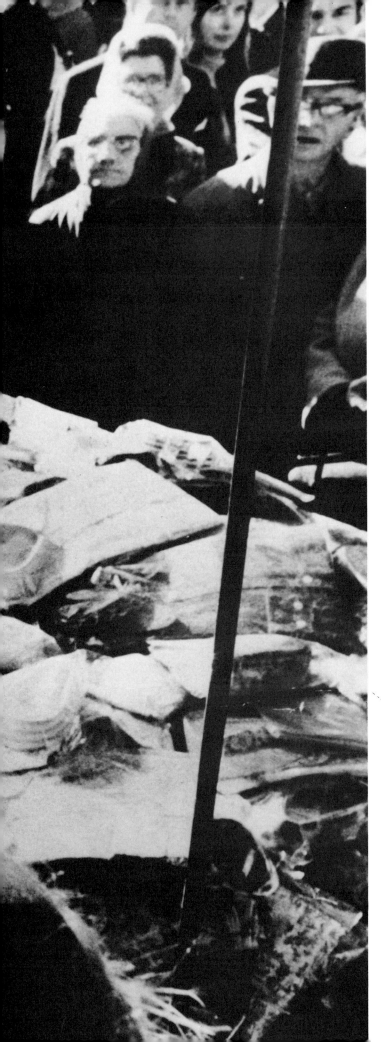

Newman had always been interested in social issues and the politics that governed the U.S. and the world. In 1970, after *Butch Cassidy*, he discovered a project that encapsulated his apprehensions about current American life. The nation was polarized. On the one hand stood the tycoons, magnates of industry, and those who served them; on the other were the revolutionaries, the activists, the hippies, the drop-outs, and the leftward-leading idealists representing these ever-spawning factions. Acquired by a temporarily expanded Rosenberg/Newman/Foreman Production Company, the script of *W.U.S.A.* dealt with the conflict between these two extremes. The tale was of an itinerant disc jockey who unwittingly becomes involved in the politics of a right-wing radio station. It was based on the novel *A Hall of Mirrors* by Robert Stone, who also wrote the screenplay.

When it was released, however, *W.U.S.A.* was disappointingly received – though not in the same fashion as previous Newman 'errors'. There were a couple of critical exceptions but, bascially, the film was attacked with a fervour unusual even by Hollywood standards. The performances by Newman, his wife Joanne, and Anthony Perkins were flawless, but the picture's tone affronted Americans and made them uncomfortable. Critics were hostile to the film's message, regarding the interpretation as hysterical and crass.

Newman was undaunted in his conviction and still regards the film as important. He went to great lengths to promote *W.U.S.A* in the face of all opposition. His strong antagonism to the 'me first' society reflected genuine concern about his country, and it dismayed him to see the film fail in its aim to bring awareness of the evils of greed and selfishness to the public. In an interview with David Frost in 1970 he explained that the purpose of this exposé of neo-fascism in America was to 'get a lot of people to ask themselves a lot of questions'.

As a film, *W.U.S.A.* took an uncompromising stand against red-neck prejudices, particularly current in the South, and it *did* rock the boat. Amongst a veritable assault on the film's faults only two reviews acknowledged the worthy motives that informed it. One of these was Vincent Canby's of the *New York Times*: 'It is not a good movie but it does, at least, prompt one to want to talk back to it – and recently there haven't been too many movies to do even that.' The other came from Frances Herridge in the *New York Post*: 'In spite of its flaws *W.U.S.A.* is one of the most provocative and relevant films this year . . . It is another joint effort of Paul Newman and his wife, Joanne Woodward, and they are both superb. So is the direction by Stuart Rosenberg . . . Pat Hingle creates an impressive atmosphere of evil power as the superpatriot, but his corrupt activities are too vaguely defined . . . it is the Newmans who carry the picture and keep it absorbing throughout . . . '

The film was certainly interesting and compelled its audiences to watch with close attention. The problem was that it was not liked and the distributors, Paramount, became antagonistic to what they had hoped would be an entertainingly controversial film and gave *W.U.S.A.* severely

On location in London for The Mackintosh Man, *1972*

limited distribution. The whole episode was hurtful to Newman, and taught him a lesson: being a superstar does not open all doors. The rules, though different, were as rigid as ever; there was a high price if you stepped out of line. And an over-emphatic political statement *was* out of line. The realization came as an unpleasant shock to him though, with characteristic bravado, he refused to be cast down.

His next film of 1970 was a further Newman/Foreman production. In a sense, *Sometimes a Great Notion* employed a similar theme to *W.U.S.A.*, that of the individual (in this case a family) who takes a stand against the prejudices of a reactionary community. The picture became Newman's second as director – once more the circumstances were accidental rather than chosen. From the beginning of production problems abounded, and Newman became dissatisfied with the director, Richard Colla. Then Newman broke his ankle and production was held up for a month. Meanwhile, disagreements multiplied and Colla quit the project. In plaster cast, Newman took over direction and restored shape and order to the runaway production.

Sometimes a Great Notion fared better than its predecessor. Again, Newman directed with flair and obtained some excellent performances. Lee Remick, who starred in the film, echoed Joanne Woodward's view of Newman's skill: 'Paul played an enormous role in the film (as well as directing it) . . . As an actress, I found his sensitivity as a director no surprise because of having worked with him as an actor, but the special understanding of actors' problems and his way of dealing with them was a great treat. It's a part of his professional life I would like to encounter again.'

Newman's forays into political controversy did not tarnish his image, however. In 1971 he was still the world's Number One Box Office Star.

In 1972, First Artists, the company founded by Newman with Poitier and Streisand in 1961, finally produced its first picture. In *Pocket Money*, he and Lee Marvin played two appealingly incompetent losers who, without success, try to hustle a living less than honestly. Although the film's theme was low-key and unspectacular, the two made a superb team; the screenplay by Terry Malick was highly skilled and in its modest fashion *Pocket Money* was a true original.

Unaccountably, the critics took a dismissive dislike to it. It was disparaged, and *Variety* declared it no more than an unsuccessful attempt to repeat the formula of *Butch Cassidy*. This was hardly just, for *Pocket Money*, with its mellow irony and lethargic, slow-witted heroes, is the antithesis of that glossy, fast-action picture.

Later in the year, First Artists' second picture was released. In *The Life and Times of Judge Roy Bean*, Newman worked with a director he had long esteemed for his individuality, John Huston. Making the film, in which Newman co-starred with an unpredictable mountain bear, was, according to the eccentric Huston, a 'romp'. For ten weeks on location in Arizona Newman appeared in virtually every scene, and he speaks of the film as 'the most delightful experience of my professional life'.

Unfortunately, the film was seriously flawed. The story of *Judge Roy Bean* was an all-American fantasy concerning a small Texas township named Langtry, after the famous Lily. Set in the late 1800s, Bean's arrival as an unwelcome stranger results in his being beaten, followed by a public hanging. A miracle occurs – the rope snaps and he survives. Later he returns in an orgy of revenge to shoot and kill all those responsible, after which he becomes the self-appointed 'judge' of the township.

Roy Bean was a role outside any previous Newman characterization – the part could have been a John Wayne classic. It was an odd choice for Newman and one can only assume that the attraction of working with Huston overrode all other considerations.

The critics expressed their disappointment and all received the film coolly. Newman had publicly declared concern for important issues on several occasions and the highly respected Pauline Kael went so far as to question his credibility over the moral issues with which the film purported to be concerned. She found the picture a simplistic right-wing fantasy whose climax was overt and mindless violence.

Not surprisingly, this second First Artists production, like the first, fared badly at the box office. Clearly Newman's coveted position as superstar was under attack.

It was the same old story all over again. In his professional career there is a constant and recurring element. With few exceptions, every success is followed by an ill-chosen failure. For every triumph, there is an artistic and commercial flop to match. The pattern is a phenomenon of his career.

In the motion picture business, failure is not usually forgiven. Most actors and actresses, once fallen, do not return to a state of grace. Yet, time and time again, Newman has done just that. Following these twin First Artists' bummers, he directed Joanne Woodward in the clumsily entitled but admirable *The Effect of Gamma Rays on the Man-in-the-Moon Marigolds*, originally a Pulitzer Prize-winning play by Paul Zindel. Miss Woodward was cast as the sluttish, gum-chewing Beatrice, whose sensitive daughter was played touchingly by the Newmans' thirteen-year-old real-life daughter, Nell.

When the film was released the critics' faith in Newman was restored and the uncompromising Pauline Kael wrote: 'He's an unobtrusive director, keeping the camera on what you'd look for in the theatre; his work is serene, sane and balanced.' All was forgiven.

And then? Newman's next film, his first of 1973, appears another act of self-indulgence. Despite their previous failure, he once more teamed up with John Huston in *The Mackintosh Man*, a slow and gloomy thriller. Presumably the two were enthused by the pleasure of each other's company, but friendship did nothing to transform this dreary project into anything more than the failure it predictably became.

Save for *The Effect of Gamma Rays*, every one of Newman's pictures since *Butch Cassidy* had been a failure. There is no question but that his box office status and bankability was now imperilled; his career was running into trouble. Yet again – and how often before had he found himself in the same situation – he needed a picture to re-establish him, but this time not only as an actor but also as a superstar.

What happened was *The Sting*. His luck is hard to credit. There is no doubt, of course, that *The Sting* was a deliberate

With daughter Nell at Sardi's. New York Critics' Awards, 1974

attempt to recreate the phenomenal success of *Butch Cassidy*, that it was produced with the express purpose of making a lot of money, that it shamelessly capitalized on an idea that was no longer original. The film is bland and cute and its story, concerning a worldly con-man and his younger, naïve sidekick, is frankly preposterous.

Yet the film's rapid-fire script, its stylish direction and slick performances, its musical score, elegant period clothes and sets, together with its dazzling pace, ensured success despite its inherent shallowness, amorality and lack of message.

And there was one other element which distinguished the movie – a factor which had not been calculated but occurred spontaneously – the film was fun to make, and that light-heartedness and pleasure shared by all involved in the production carries over to the screen.

Audiences paid no attention whatsoever to the critics' carping at the picture. That it lacked depth or was cynically motivated was irrelevant: they adored it. It became a giant success at the box office, its clothes and music became a cult.

What made it was what made *Butch Cassidy*, the pure magic of the relationship between Redford and Newman. The love affair proved even better the second time around.

Right: With Eileen Brennan on the set of The Sting, *1973*

Page 96: World favourite actor and actress (Natalie Wood). Golden Globe Awards 1959

Page 97: Directing Estelle Parsons in Rachel, Rachel, *1968*

94

9
A MAN UNTO HIMSELF

Paul Newman is possessed of that rare quality among human beings: charm. He has a compelling attraction for all kinds of people, whatever their sex or social standing. As an actor he appeals to every sort of audience, all of whom find something with which they can identify.

Unlike many actors, he does not court popularity. Because of a stubborn refusal to be other than himself, he commands genuine respect, both as man and as actor – rare in the world where respect is hard to win and usually lasts only as long as the reviews remain favourable.

For some, he is the thinking man's hero, an individual who possesses that compelling synthesis of a resolute, almost sexual, toughness and creative intelligence. Intellectual French movie buffs adore him. Analytical film periodicals, with their love of the obscure but meaningful, devote as much attention to dissecting his art as that of Louis Malle or Federico Fellini. They recognize the intelligence of their hero and note with satisfaction how this is employed in his work.

For others, Newman is a macho legend, the street-wise tough guy with rough and ready principles. For them he is the stud, the daring go-getter, the kind of man they would like to be.

And for women everwhere Newman is a sex symbol – although he loathes this aspect of his appeal. However, it was always unavoidable. How could a man of such good looks, tempered by the cynical directness of the eyes, with such warmth of character, not be sexually attractive? Newman's appeal lies in his capacity to appear both mean and tender at the same time. His long and happy marriage to Joanne Woodward only adds to his allure – not only is he beautiful, he is honourable as well. His pride in her, their, shared career and six children – surely these reveal another important virtue? Clearly he knows how to keep a woman happy. To Newman's embarrassment, this huge female following on one occasion publicly proclaimed their convictions – by voting him the man they would most like to take to bed.

For almost all who see Newman, whether on screen or in person, the most striking impression is of his presence and physical superiority. With the passing of time his looks merely improve. Always in glowing health, the fine lines and greying hair have added dignity to that youthful strength of his features. His body is taut and lithe, that of a man many years younger. Always energetic, he remains fit and exercises regularly to combat his only negative tendency – a beer belly.

Newman is also well-loved within his profession. David Niven spoke for many when expressing his appreciation: 'He is a dedicated professional, totally understanding and generous in his work with others, has a wild sense of humour and somehow manages to consume enormous quantities of beer without putting on a single ounce! It is a lasting disgrace that this splendid actor, for some reason, has not yet been awarded an Oscar. He has done more good for Hollywood movies and therefore for the world of films than anyone else I can think of since the great studios virtually collapsed.'

Newman never ceases to be bewildered by the response he arouses in people. It embarrasses him; he feels it has no relevance to his job and has never considered he owes anything to his admirers apart from delivering the best of his craft. There is a certain naïveté in this, for his charisma is spell-binding. He does not seem to comprehend that the more elusive and self-effacing he becomes, the more attention he excites. He does not see the paradox. He is impatient with this adoration and familiarity from strangers, applying the same harsh standards in his judgement of their behaviour as he would to someone close to him who took similar liberties.

He does not like reporters and is particularly ill at ease with female journalists – against whom he armours himself resolutely. He is polite but hostile when asked the same old questions. Attempts to discuss his blue eyes incense him. Probing questions on his private life are answered with the minimum of information.

While it may well be frustrating for journalists and columnists, Newman's refusal to share his private life with the public can only be regarded as admirable, for many actors lacking in his maturity thrive on such attentions. They relish gossip, baring their souls and telling all to the Press. Without criticizing, Newman considers such self-exposure undignified and unworthy.

Infringements on his privacy Newman regards as an unacceptable violation, and he guards his private and family life jealously. He will not sign autographs, considering the practice as the worst sort of vanity. Not even the most beguiling request will alter his resolve, although he will go to great lengths to explain gently and politely to a disappointed child why this is so.

After *Butch Cassidy and the Sundance Kid* and, later, *The*

At Bridgehampton Races, 1981

Sting had given him superstar status, Newman's life became more and more affected by the demands and attentions of the Press, the public and the business. No longer was it just the fans who made every public appearance a torture. Now he was also sought out by every sycophant in the industry, and even in the blasé and sophisticated film world his presence caused a stir. Wherever he went, attention focused upon him and his entourage. Strangers interrupted conversations, distant acquaintances claimed intimate familiarity. In work, too, the pressure mounted. He was bombarded with scripts and offers. Often it became intolerable.

Whenever possible Newman retreats, together with his family, to his rambling coach-house near Westport, Connecticut. Here the family can live like the normal people which, in spite of everything, they are. Westport is their true home, where the Newmans planted their roots many years ago. After the unreal existence he is obliged to live out in New York and Hollywood, Newman takes refuge in family life, which is where he feels most at ease. In a house full of children and countless animals, in a setting of rural beauty and surrounded by a loyal community, he can believe that, after all, it has all been worth it.

Although Newman is reticent about his role as family man and rarely discusses his children, they are clearly more important to him than anything else. Only within the bosom of his tribe does he relax completely, take off his shoes and lounge in front of the television with the inevitable beer at hand.

He says, 'I don't spend as much time with my children as some fathers, but when I am with them I enjoy it, and so do they. But I don't have a lot of patience. They know that, and they try me. But at a given point they flee in terror!'

But his bright and unspoiled offspring are a testimony to both Newman's and Joanne's successful efforts to bring them up as normally as possible. He is proud of them and misses them when he is away. Not infrequently, he takes the entire brood out to eat in a restaurant and the noisy ease and affection that flows between father and children is endearingly evident.

What Newman has always valued most highly in life is freedom and involvement in exhilarating work or play, whatever he chose. Fame has never been his goal in life, only a solid reputation and a degree of financial security.

By the time he reached his forties, Newman had acquired all the things that most men only dream of, and had done so with no residual stain upon his conscience. There are no snide tales of what he did to achieve success. His moral balance sheet is faultless. An honourable marriage, a refusal to conform to any other than his own high ethical standards, a strong sense of justice that he is not afraid to demonstrate by supporting his less fortunate fellow men, years of solid achievement – all these combine to make him, in middle age, a responsible, sincere and stable personality.

Perhaps the most striking of Newman's qualities is his humanitarianism. In the glossy world of Hollywood it is almost impossible not to lose some degree of idealism. The inhabitants move in a world so highly competitive, so relentlessly geared to profit and material success, that little energy or interest remains for the world outside. A social

Father and daughter, Melissa, 1969

Right: Susan Newman
Far right: Newman with daughters Melissa and Nell
Below: The reluctant sex symbol in bed with his wife

conscience inevitably becomes blunted as, for most who are part of it, there is no other world. Hollywood takes itself deadly seriously.

Newman's feelings for the city that helped to make him are well known. He detests it. He was never spiritually a part of it. Partly, it has to do with intelligence, this ability to remain alert, aware and principled. From a young man with a high I.Q. and inherent curiosity he has always been involved with social issues and interested in politics. He publicly declared his opposition to America's intervention in the Vietnam war in 1962, a year later demonstrating his concern by taking part in the Civil Rights march on Washington. In that same year, he and fellow artists Marlon Brando and Tony Franciosa, among others, travelled to Gadsden, Alabama, in an attempt to promote racial harmony. The actors were made unwelcome in no uncertain terms – the mayor of Gadsden refused to meet this mission from Hollywood, labelling them 'rabble-rousers'. Race relations were so bad that only a handful of blacks greeted their arrival with enthusiasm and Newman was disappointed to have achieved so little.

Later, when Martin Luther King was murdered, Newman, together with Brando, took to the streets in protest and once again was dismayed by the apathy shown towards such vital issues by his fellow citizens – apart from the very young who were beginning seriously to question the attitudes of their elders. Yet while everyone else complained that America was falling apart, no one could remain unaware of the country's hidden third world – those ghastly ghettoes of the poor in every major city. Millions of

Americans were underprivileged in every sense of the word: financially, culturally, environmentally, educationally and in health. In a country that worshipped success above all, too many people got stepped upon and left behind.

Both Newman and his wife were acutely conscious of these injustices. Their views, which they aired publicly, proved unpopular with the Hollywood establishment, who preferred their stars to be apolitical and to offend no one.

Later in the 1960s, Newman became even more actively involved in politics. In the presidential campaign of 1968 he supported Eugene McCarthy, whom he greatly admired for his courage and almost singlehanded opposition to President Johnson's war policies. He campaigned on college campuses and in his own community in Connecticut, and this work taught him a good deal about the realities of politics, how idealism in itself is not enough for the achievement of social progress. 'The memory of that campaign,' he told journalist Michael Billington of *The Times* in 1969, 'is rather like a low-relief map of the Pyrenees; everything has been flattened out, it was so hectic. It left one with an awareness, however, that transitional phases are slow and awkward and that one can't go from machine politics to participatory democracy in a night. The machine is a lot tougher and smellier than one ever thought it would be.'

During the McCarthy campaign Newman broke his own

Left: Campaigning for Eugene McCarthy, 1968

Below: Broadway for Peace. With Senator Wayne Morris and Harry Belafonte, the same year

rule by signing autographs, for had he not he would have gained enemies in lieu of supporters. He came into close contact with the man and woman in the street and for him the experience was sometimes moving.

'The thing I'll always remember about that whole McCarthy campaign,' says Newman, 'was this cop in New Hampshire. We were going somewhere with a police escort, and one of the cops pointed to his partner and said he'd received word the night before that his son had been killed in Vietnam . . . The man's son was dead, and that was a hell of a thing to put against political theory . . . I offered the cop my sympathy, and he thanked me. Then we stood there. Finally I blurted out something: what did he think about some creep, some Hollywood peacenik, a functioning illiterate, coming in there and telling him about the war? And the cop said, no, he didn't resent what I was doing. Even if a war takes your boy, he said, that doesn't make it right.'

Following the McCarthy campaign, Newman lent his active support to Joseph Duffy, national chairman of Americans for Democratic Action, in his campaign as candidate for the Senate. On another occasion, in 1970, campaigning for Pete McCloskey in California, he made fifty-three speeches in just three days.

Throughout the 1960s and early 1970s, Newman was active in his support of left-wing causes. Some of the more sombre political activists mocked his motives, and by these the Newmans and their circle were disparaged as the creators of 'radical chic'. Others, however, had no doubts about their sincerity and in 1969 the Newmans received the William J. German Human Relations Award of the American Jewish Committee.

'This may come as a surprise,' Newman told Charles Hamblett, the author, 'but I'm not really anti-establishment. I'm absolutely square. I'm anti-idiocy, anti-dishonesty – and the motion picture industry as a whole has its roots in dishonesty . . .'

Now Newman has withdrawn somewhat from that world. 'What's happened to me in a political sense,' he explains, 'is that I've gotten tired . . . Jane Fonda is probably a little more radical than I am, although not all that much . . . Jane's committed herself to an action position a lot more than I have. Trying to have visibility without being visible has always been my impulse. The main distinction between Jane and me, I think, is that she enjoys it – she enjoys the hassle. Me, I never enjoyed the hassle. Making speeches, shaking hands, dealing with the Press – it's all a pain in the ass . . . which is why I wouldn't ever get into politics. It would drive me *wild*.'

When Newman began to make real money he started his own trust fund, the No Such Foundation. The Foundation contributed to causes he believed in, such as the Civil Rights Movement. Another major contribution was in support of the Centre for the Study of Democratic Institutions. This organisation, founded in 1959 with a $4 million grant from the Ford Foundation is situated in Santa Barbara, California, and, with running costs of $1 million per year, relies entirely on charitable donations. Other film personalities such as Kirk Douglas, Jack Lemmon and Steve Allen are among its patrons. Its aims are, in loose terms, to examine and anticipate change and development in America. These studies are not restricted to political and social changes but extend to subjects such as the inevitability of increasing leisure time and how this may most productively be utilized in human terms. The Centre holds regular seminars at which anyone can join sociologists, scientists, psychologists and mathematicians in discussing important issues of the day.

Newman frequently attends these gatherings and continues in his support for the Centre's work. His commitment remains undimmed for, above the narrow factionalism of party politics, he believes the more fortunate of the population have a duty to improve an imperfect world.

The casualty rate among those in the film industry is notoriously high. Newman has survived and prospered, achieving a reputation, both on screen and off, that is universally admired.

It has been observed that he has always been blessed with more than his fair share of good fortune. *Somebody Up There Likes Me*, the title of his second picture, has followed him as a catch phrase throughout his later life.

But that benevolent good fortune did not last forever. At the age of fifty-three his luck broke. Despite the apparent solidity of all he had achieved, in the later 1970s Newman experienced the worst period of his life, both professionally and, even more painfully, within his family.

It would be his spirit's lowest ebb.

Right: With Warren Beatty at 'Together for McGovern', Madison Square Garden, 1972

Page 108: At Cool Hand Luke *première party, 1967*

Page 109: Well . . . the eyes still have it. (An unusual study of Newman in the National Enquirer, *1975)*

10
THE BAD YEARS

The year 1974 began promisingly enough for Newman. Untypically, he moved straight from one huge commercial hit, *The Sting*, into another. *The Towering Inferno*, while considered questionable in terms of taste and artistic merit, was nevertheless a staggeringly successful film at the box office. The public had been lured away from their television sets by a new cinematic phenomenon – the disaster movie.

In the early 1970s, the industry produced a spate of sensationalist films which blatantly exploited the voyeurism existing, to some extent, in all of us. Playing on a universal compulsion to linger over tragedy and catastrophe, whether this be the ten-car pile up, the severing of limbs by mythical beasts, or the sight of ectoplasm spewing from the mouths of the possessed, cinemas attracted record audiences with such pictures as *Jaws, Earthquake* and *The Exorcist*.

Exploiting the trend, 20th Century-Fox and Warner Brothers discovered they were both preparing a movie on the same theme and decided to pool their not inconsiderable resources. Based on two novels, *The Towering Inferno* was to be the ultimate in disaster pictures.

The film was stacked with big names and established stars. Apart from Newman, who plays the architect of a high-rise block with inadequate fire precautions, the cast included Steve McQueen, Faye Dunaway and Robert Wagner, with the nostalgia-provoking addition of Fred Astaire and Jennifer Jones.

Although *The Towering Inferno* was a superior example of the genre (the story was at least believable and the movie was responsible for the renewal and modernization of fire equipment all over the country), it nevertheless fell into the same trap as most such pictures. In an effort to draw massive audiences, star performers were contracted to play even minor roles. Yet so many guest appearances only served to diminish the impact and stature of the individual stars.

Although Newman's was a major role, this was devalued by the all-star cast and obscured by the sheer technical effect of the raging inferno itself. He delivered an adequate performance but, inevitably, did not appear as much in control as usual, which indeed he was not, and occasionally seemed distinctly uncomfortable in his part.

A factor that the film-makers had failed to take into account was that extreme and violent catastrophe finally numbs the sense of its audiences. Hence the craze for these films was short-lived.

However, *The Towering Inferno* appeared at a time when the formula was still effective. It was hugely popular and the film made Newman a great deal of money personally.

But this was not a good time to mount worthwhile pictures. In its attempt to produce films that either shocked or terrified, the industry became unadventurous as it clung to a misjudged conviction that disasters were the only movies that audiences would leave their homes to see. All the better films to appear at this time were independently produced.

Newman, in spite of his reputation, was not unaffected by this barren atmosphere. By 1975 he had already started filming on his next picture, *The Drowning Pool*, supposedly a sequel to the highly successful but ten-year-old *Harper*. Ideas really were thin on the ground.

The Drowning Pool was rewarded for its lack of originality by deservedly poor reviews, the one saving grace being Joanne Woodward's performance in a part neither large nor challenging enough.

This picture marked the beginning of a serious decline in Newman's career and popularity during the remainder of the 1970s, though this was not immediately apparent. The couple were as fêted as ever, lending their name and influence to fund-raising rallies and a campaign against off-shore oil drilling in California, and appearing at various conferences. Together they made a documentary on ecology, and Newman also finished creditably in several motor races, the sport he had by now embraced.

From the outside it all look good. But then, suddenly and unexpectedly, the couple found themselves under savage attack from the media. Never enjoying a comfortable relationship with the Press at the best of times, Newman now found himself in a situation where many took their revenge for his long-standing rejection of them. For years the gossip columnists had willed disaster on this so perfect couple, whose marriage, they felt, had gone on quite long enough.

Now, without warning, vicious and unsubstantiated reports commented on every so-called negative aspect of the Newman marriage. Their different tastes and interests were

Outside the Beverly Hills Hotel, 1975

interpreted and reported as disharmony. A single row in public at Sardi's in New York was blown up out of all proportion. The Newmans had had it, they were finished. A comment of Joanne's in an interview the previous year was used to add fuel to the campaign. She had said that she and Newman had given up a double and now slept in twin beds. Had the reasons for this been anything other than practical it is hardly likely that the proud and dignified Miss Woodward would have announced it quite so publicly. The Press, however, were resistant to any logic. The absurd episode became a nightmare and Newman's efforts to refute lies and distortions were rewarded only when the story had run its course.

To be realistic, the Newmans of course do have their differences. They row like any other couple, though perhaps less often. Both believe in clearing the air. After so many years of marriage neither is threatened by displays of anger from the other. Both are assertive, strong and intelligent individuals and with each other they feel confident in expressing disagreement. They regard their occasional altercations as a healthy aspect of their union. 'I am all in favour of a good screaming free-for-all every two or three months,' Newman told journalist Jane Wilson, 'it clears the air, gets rid of old grievances . . . ' The marriage has contained snappy, less-than-contented episodes, but both know when to start listening and to take note. The partnership is without a destructive pattern. Each respects the other deeply.

In 1976 Newman embarked upon one of the most disastrous associations of his career. Furthermore, as earlier with John Huston, he seemed determined to continue with the partnership after it had proved a failure.

This partner was Robert Altman, a brilliant director and *auteur* responsible for such films as *Three Women*, *Nashville* and *The Wedding*. Altman was so observant, intelligent and original in technique that some felt he approached genius. This same talent, however, created a few irritating, perverse and almost insane pictures. The chaotic *Brewster McCloud* is one such example.

Altman was justly renowned for his off-beat successes, however, and it is understandable that Newman should have been inspired by the prospect of working with a director whose approach to film-making was so refreshingly different. The two men became close friends and Newman's eldest daughter, Susan, appeared in Altman's superb *The Wedding*.

Their first venture together, Newman's follow-up to *The Drowning Pool*, was the self-consciously titled *Buffalo Bill and the Indians, Or Sitting Bull's History Lesson*. The Newman/Foreman company had acquired the original play *Indians*, by Arthur Kopit, back in 1969, but nothing had ever come of it. For reasons known only to himself, Newman had dredged up this old property as the first vehicle for the Newman/Altman team.

Buffalo Bill and the Indians is a long, repetitive work which exposes the myths that surround a hero and the convention representing Red Indians as 'baddies'. The script was weak to begin with, and the announcement in the credits that it had been loosely adapted from the play was a forewarning of two hours of incoherence.

Newman himself was good in the role of Buffalo Bill,

giving his character dignity and humanity, but the film emerged as one of the most dismal flops of his career to date. After only one week a London cinema asked for the film to be taken off, so bad was the response. Newman had never known such devastating failure in his work.

That same year – again an indication of his obsession to do anything different – he accepted a small cameo role in Mel Brooks 'Silent Movie*. The picture was full of these star appearances and Newman's was without dialogue. In America, his name did not even appear on the film's posters.

In the spring of 1977, Joanne was cast opposite Laurence Olivier in a British production of William Inge's *Come Back Little Sheba*. This opportunity came at a favourable moment, for Miss Woodward, as gifted and strong-willed as her husband, was suffering from living under his shadow. She did not hold him personally responsible – he had always tried to share everything with her – and Newman himself understood her need to be judged on her own unique merits. Joanne was desperate for a little independence in which to express her neglected identity. In one wistful remark during an interview at the time she summed up her dilemma: 'The only time I'm recognized in public is when I'm with Paul,' she said. 'Even then, people aren't looking at me. They're looking at him.'

The trip to work in England presented itself as the answer. She would extend her visit after filming and spend a year away. Meanwhile, the stereotype of Mr and Mrs Perfect would be broken. Newman would look after their three daughters, a task he anticipated with the same enthusiasm as he did any new venture. It was not a separation. The couple would see each other frequently during the year and then resume their life together. It was not a split-up, though the episode was another of the life changes that Newman experienced in the late 1970s.

Made during that same year, Newman's next film salvaged some of the damage done to his career though in role it was merely a return to the reliable old format.

Slapshot was an ice-hockey drama distinctive for its frequent use of foul language. Despite some criticism for this, the picture, though not always convincing, was exciting and entertaining. It was the first Newman film since *The Towering Inferno* to do well at the box office. *Slapshot* proved, at the very least, that he was still capable of turning out a solid performance of the kind audiences would pay to see. But he had given better, much better, and he knew it.

And then he did something he had never done before in his professional life. He made a break from it, and it is typical of Newman that this sabbatical took the form not of rest but instead a wholehearted involvement in his new passion, motor racing. It was an escape into a simpler if infinitely more dangerous world, a world in which he was no longer a celebrity but merely 'one of the boys'. Yet even into this new setting the dark fates pursued him.

In December 1978, Newman's only son, Scott, died in a Los Angeles motel at the age of twenty-eight. The death was caused by an overdose of alcohol and drugs and was believed to be accidental. It was a tragic ending to a sad young life. Newman, to whom his children were of the utmost importance and whom he loved without reservation, was

As Buffalo Bill in Robert Altman's Buffalo Bill and the Indians, *1976*

numbed by shock and grief. There can be no greater loss than that of a first-born son.

Scott Newman's death had been precipitated by many years of emotional conflict accompanied by a serious drink problem. In 1974 he had been arrested and released on bail after being charged with battery, disturbing the peace, malicious mischief and destruction of jail property. The episode in itself was no more serious than the occasional brawls his father had participated in as a young man, but Scott had begun to combine alcohol with valium and the various other drugs prescribed for him.

While Newman, his first wife and Miss Woodward had done all possible to ease the trauma of divorce for the children, and subsequently made every effort to protect them, Scott had always been the most vulnerable. Seven years old at the time of his parents' break-up, he was more aware of it and thus more affected than the others. As the only boy in the family, his identification with his father was necessarily more intense than that of his five sisters. By the time he was nine, rival siblings were being born and access to his father, already restricted by the nature of their living arrangements, was further hampered by the demands of a second growing family requiring similar attention.

Though separated, his mother and father did everything in their power to make Scott feel special and secure but, from early childhood, he had been aware that his father was unique, successful and popular. Consequently, as he grew up, he could not help but observe his exceptionally attractive and clever parent receiving attentions that detracted from his own special need for recognition. As Scott became older, this unpleasant awareness intensified and as a young man he saw that much was expected of him simply because he was his father's son.

Newman Senior was sympathetic to his son's dilemma, encouraged him to follow the paths he wanted, and refrained from adding further pressure. But the world outside was where Scott would have to establish his own identity and it was there that this attitude was prevalent. It is notoriously hard for sons of highly successful and charismatic men to escape a sense of failure and to feel confident that they are as good as others. From childhood onwards there is often an uncomfortable sense of being in a race they cannot win. Scott Newman was a classic victim of this situation. He was doomed to live in the shadow of his famous parents, however hard he tried to find his own place in the sun.

While he was never tempted to follow his father into a career in acting, Scott did, however, appear in small roles in *The Towering Inferno* and *The Great Waldo Pepper* (starring Robert Redford), but he was more interested in the technical effects and mechanics of film-making. He toyed with the idea of becoming a stunt man and, as a fearless and extremely competent skydiver, he would have found little difficulty in establishing himself.

But depression was by now a chronic problem and, when he realized the depth of this affliction, Newman Senior sought the best treatment available in an attempt to help his unhappy son. But by then it seemed the state of mind was too deeply ingrained. During the last months before his death Scott was working in a nightclub under an assumed

A pensive Scott Newman with his father and stepmother in 1968

name, in an effort to hide his connection with his famous father. It was the final denial.

Newman was overcome by grief over his son's death. Even Scott's sense of failure could not have matched his own at the time. When he received the news of his son's death he was at his old college, Kenyon, directing students in a new play by Michael Cristofer called *C. C. Pyle and the Bunion Derby.*

Hardly able to absorb the news, Newman assembled his young cast and said, 'It would help me if you'd all be as rowdy as possible.' That night the students dressed up in funny clothes as if for a celebratory wake and took a case of beer and a bottle of Scotch to Newman's room. He took a long pull at the whisky and then smiled at his visitors. 'It's the first time I've touched hard stuff in eight years,' he confided. Then he gently and affectionately bade them goodnight and closed the door. It was his longest, loneliest night ever.

After Scott's death Newman threw himself into work, the most difficult but most effective way of combating great unhappiness. In 1979 he made another picture with Robert Altman, in defiance of their previous disaster. It was vital to keep busy, and to work with an understanding friend made the task more palatable.

Why the unquestionable individual talents of Newman and Altman did not succeed together is not easy to understand. Altman is an imaginative and sensitive director and Newman an adaptable and intelligent interpreter of ideas. Their combined resources should have produced some kind of magic but they did not. *Quintet* was an abysmal, futuristic film, set in a frozen world, the human story laced with homosexual undertones. The picture was so obscure and poorly received and its release and distribution so limited, that mercifully few people have ever been exposed to it.

Newman followed this awful picture with a flop of such proportions that it looked as though there existed no further depths for him to fall. Irwin Allen's *When Time Ran Out* was intended to be the disaster movie of all time and, in a sense, it was, for the result was so appalling that even with a supporting cast including William Holden and Jackie Bisset it achieved the almost impossible – reviews and reactions worse than those for *Buffalo Bill and the Indians.*

It was the cruel finale to years of both personal and public unhappiness, strain, failure and the decline of a hard-won reputation. Always surviving the bad times, none had been as bad as these last few years.

As the 1970s came to an end and a new decade began, it appeared inconceivable that Paul Newman should ever recapture the renown and bankability or regain the eminence he once had known.

In Robert Altman's Quintet, *1979*

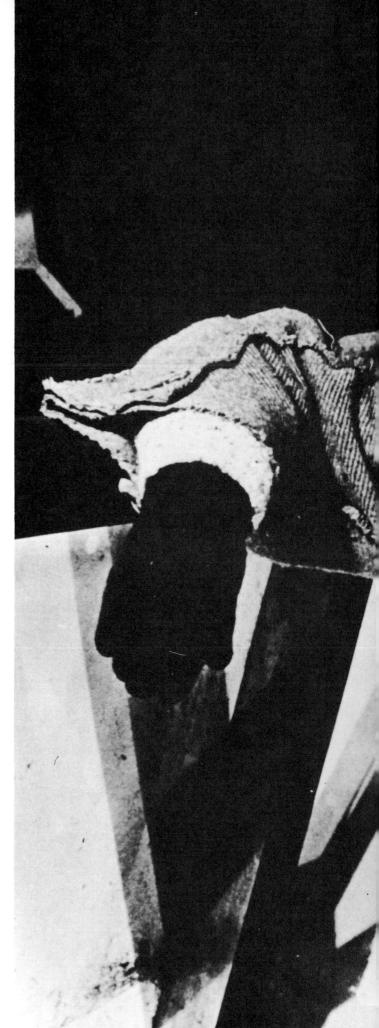

Left: Mr and Mrs Newman leaving the Circle Theater where Joanne was appearing in Candida, *1981*

Far left: In When Time Ran Out, *1980*

Below: Leaving the wrap-up party for King of the Gypsies, *1978*

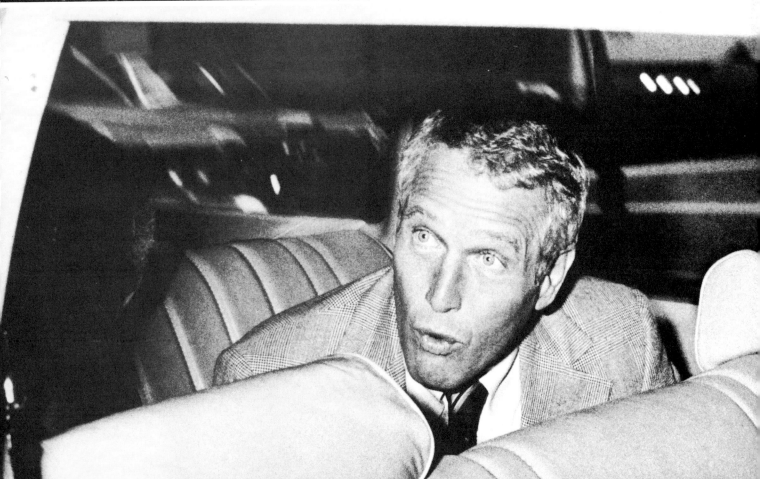

11
THE RACING DRIVER

The death of his son left Newman devastated. It was some months before he was able to speak openly of the tragedy.

Apart from this sadness in his personal life, his career, too, had left him jaded and disillusioned. A series of, at best, indifferent films over the past few years had dulled the enthusiasm that had sustained him for so long. He had always hated being a celebrity and now it had become more meaningless than ever. His once-committed search for new and inspiring roles had lost its urgency. Too many of his sometimes reckless forays into the unknown had led to no more than a confirmation of his failure to get out of a rut. Newman had questioned the ultimate value of his craft on many previous occasions – a comment from an interview several years earlier in which he described acting as 'stupid, silly and nothing to do with being an adult' was endlessly re-quoted – but this time it was serious. His energy had run out; he was tired and faced an uncertain future.

In short, he had become bored with acting and weary of the industry. Yet though he would never entirely recover from his loss, once the reactive depression that was its consequence had run its course, Newman faced up to life once more. It was not long before he had flung himself back into the rigours of film-making and, despite the resounding failure of *Quintet* and *When Time Ran Out*, simply to work became a therapy.

More effective still, another occupation altogether had grown to dominate his life and into this he now sublimated his frustrations and his grief. What had started as a hobby had developed into a consuming interest, and Newman poured all the energy previously reserved for acting into the sport that virtually had become his new career.

Newman's enthusiasm for cars and racing driving had started late, although he had always harboured a passion for speed and an interest in the mechanics of high-powered engines. Even as a young man, the looks of a car were immaterial to him and – unusual among his peers – he chose to drive unostentatious and frequently beat-up automobiles which he discarded only when they were ready for the scrap heap.

However his love of speed could not be satisfied by this type of car and, in 1961, he compromised by fitting a Porsche engine into his Volkswagen. Working in New York at the time, the souped-up Volkswagen cut his journey home to Connecticut by an hour. Driving fast became a keen pleasure and soon he acquired the habit of spending time on whichever professional circuit was closest to where he was working. He grew to like the racing world and the men who inhabited it and, whenever possible, would arrange his film commitment to enable him to attend the Indianapolis 500-mile race.

But his real commitment to racing did not form until 1969, while making *Winning*. The action of the film centred on Indianapolis and, determined to dispense with a double, he enrolled at Bob Bondurant's school.

Bob Bondurant, ace racing coach and champion driver over two decades, at once noticed Newman's instinctive flair behind the wheel. Literally returning to the classroom – practice on the track came only later – Bondurant taught him the theory and fundamentals of competitive racing. Moving on to accompany his coach in a car, learning basic positioning, then taking the wheel himself, in less than a week Newman advanced to handle a Lola 270, a Ford Grand National stock car and a Ford GT40, all normally driven only by professionals. Racing was second nature to him; within a few months he had progressed to competition standard.

Bondurant's training prepared him for *Winning*, where on and off camera at Indianapolis he demonstrated his freshly-honed skills and dispensed with the professional driver chosen to double for him – causing near heart attacks in his producers.

Bondurant's training also provided him with the confidence to pursue the sport after filming was completed. He became fascinated by the details of that world – who had won what, where, when and how – and soon was an acknowledged expert on the subject, a natural choice as narrator for ABC-TV's special *Once Upon a Wheel* in 1971. As a driver however, competent as he was, there was still much to learn. It was not until four years after *Winning* that

Newman rests his helmet on top of the Datsun which he drove to victory at Lime Rock Park in 1980

Newman finally gained the special licence required for competition racing.

Meanwhile, he practised whenever he could find a track at hand. He spent more and more time at the auto club at Lime Rock, close to his home in Connecticut. In 1973, he passed some months in England making *The Mackintosh Man* with John Huston. By now his name was familiar to many in the racing world – not as an actor, but as a driver. During breaks in filming Newman could be found at Brands Hatch, perfecting his technique in a Formula Ford provided for him by the Ford Motor Company for the duration of his visit. Usually easy-going on film sets, the largely British cast and crew found him pleasant but reserved. This was perhaps due to the unfamiliar surroundings and working with people previously unknown to him. However, when talking about his new passion, they noticed that he became transformed. There was a quality of the delicacy, power, precise control,

and sheer mechanical beauty of high speed cars which sparked something in his heart. He became filled with boyish enthusiasm whenever the subject came up.

But it was not until he was almost fifty – an old man by racing standards – that Newman began competing in amateur races. After his first few races he had acquired the nickname 'Old Balloon Foot' – an allusion to a fault he had not yet overcome – but soon the edge, determination and love of challenge, that had been put to such good use before, was directed into this new area. Newman now demonstrated to even the most exacting of the experts that his skill on the track was the result of more than enthusiasm. He became as dedicated in his pursuit for excellence in this greasy, exacting, no bullshit society, as ever he had been in the tinselled milieu from whence he came.

In 1977 his career took off. He won two national championship races driving a Datsun, and coming first was one of the best moments of his life. 'I remember the first race I ever won,' he recalls, 'the sheer joy was worth all the Oscars in the world.'

Though filming kept him from the track longer than he cared for, Newman started increasingly to organize his time and commitments around racing events. He began to accumulate an impressive list of victories and achievements. His obsession had become well-known to his friends in the film industry, and some were bemused by his fondness for a world so totally different from their own. Others – Steve McQueen, Clint Eastwood, James Garner and David Carradine among them – shared and understood the lure of an existence that, to them, held more genuine excitement, risk, challenge and indeed true glamour than all the shadowplay of Hollywood.

They admired him for entering the sport so late yet demonstrating such guts and dedication. Others were not beyond teasing a little. Robert Redford had promised to give him a Porsche for his fiftieth birthday in 1975. The day arrived, and sure enough, a Porsche – of a kind – was delivered to Newman's home. Ancient, battered and

Left: With the late Graham Hill, 1974

Below: Newman relaxing with Pancho Gonzalez in Ontario, California, 1970

Following page: The Racing Driver. Newman comes in first at Lime Rock Park, 1980

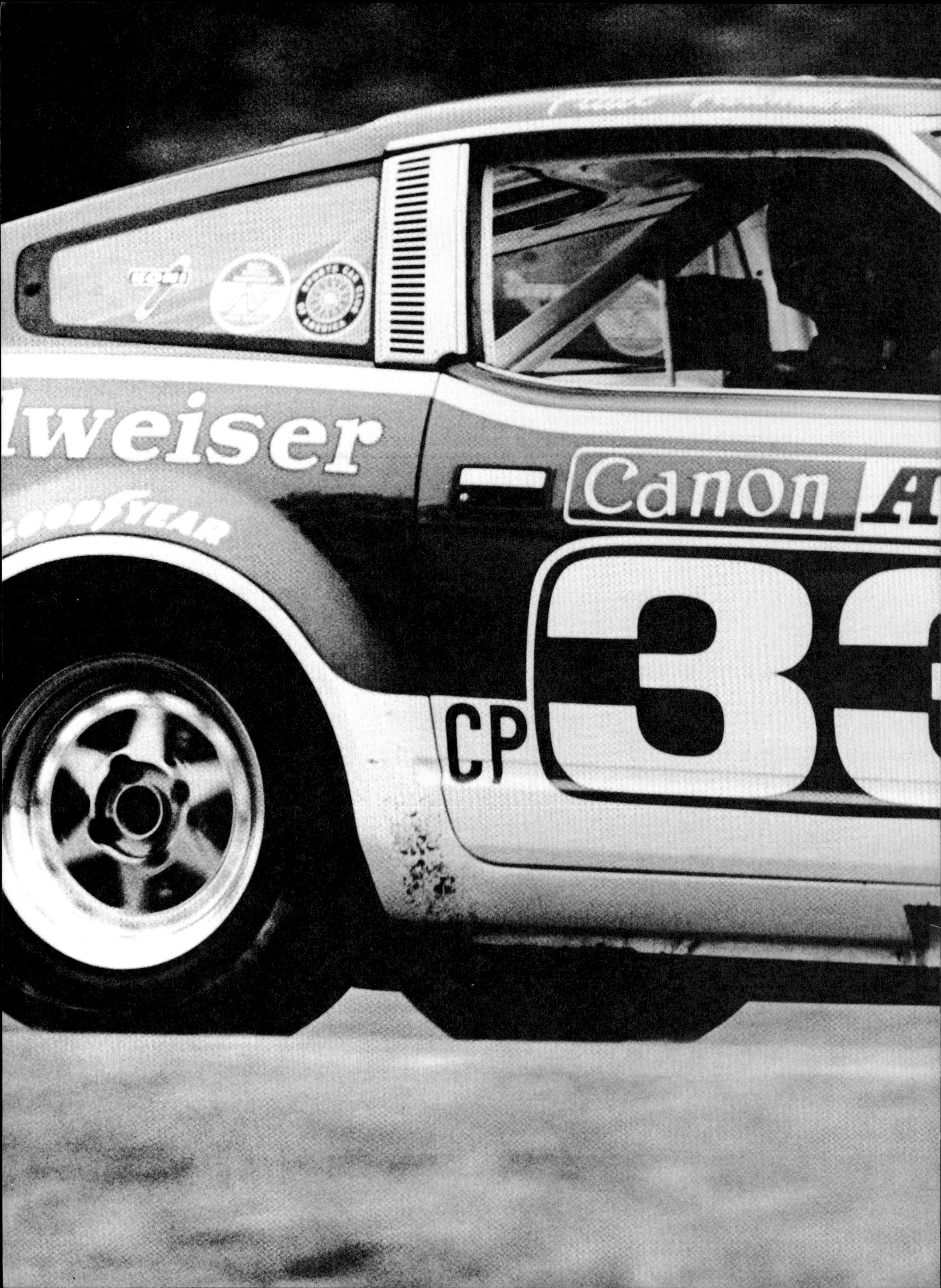
Canon
GOODYEAR
CP

engineless, Redford had bought it from a scrap heap for a few dollars. Not to be outdone, Newman arranged for the wreck to be compressed into a neat but immensely heavy cube which was dumped on Redford's porch.

By 1977 Newman was established as a competitor to be reckoned with. Experts in the sport acknowledged his instinctive flair and consider that he would undoubtedly have become a top Grand Prix driver, had he started younger. Whilst at first insisting that he raced cars purely for pleasure and claiming disinterest in the competitive aspect, over the years Newman has changed his attitude. His name and achievements are conspicuous in the field since his first wins in 1974.

In 1975, he formed his own team: P.L.N. Racing. A year later he became national champion in Class D (for small sports cars: Newman drove a Triumph TR-6) production racing. He also came third overall in Class B sedan racing

(saloons) driving a Datsun 510. In the latter half of the 1970s Newman won all the four Sports Car Club of America races he entered, again driving Datsuns. In one of these he set a new track record at Watkins Glen in upstate New York.

In April 1977, driving a Ferrari, Newman's team took part in the Daytona twenty-four-hour Endurance Race and came in a creditable fifth, beating professionals like Jochen Mass. That same season he competed in the twelve-hour Endurance Race at Sebring, Florida, in a Porsche 911S which was plagued with clutch and gear trouble and finished way behind the leading cars. However, the following year he and his team won twelve of the fifteen races they entered.

Below: Newman gives daughter Claire the winner's kiss at Lime Rock Park, 1980

Right: Usually a beer man, Newman the victor gets his teeth into a bottle of champagne at Lime Rock Park, 1980

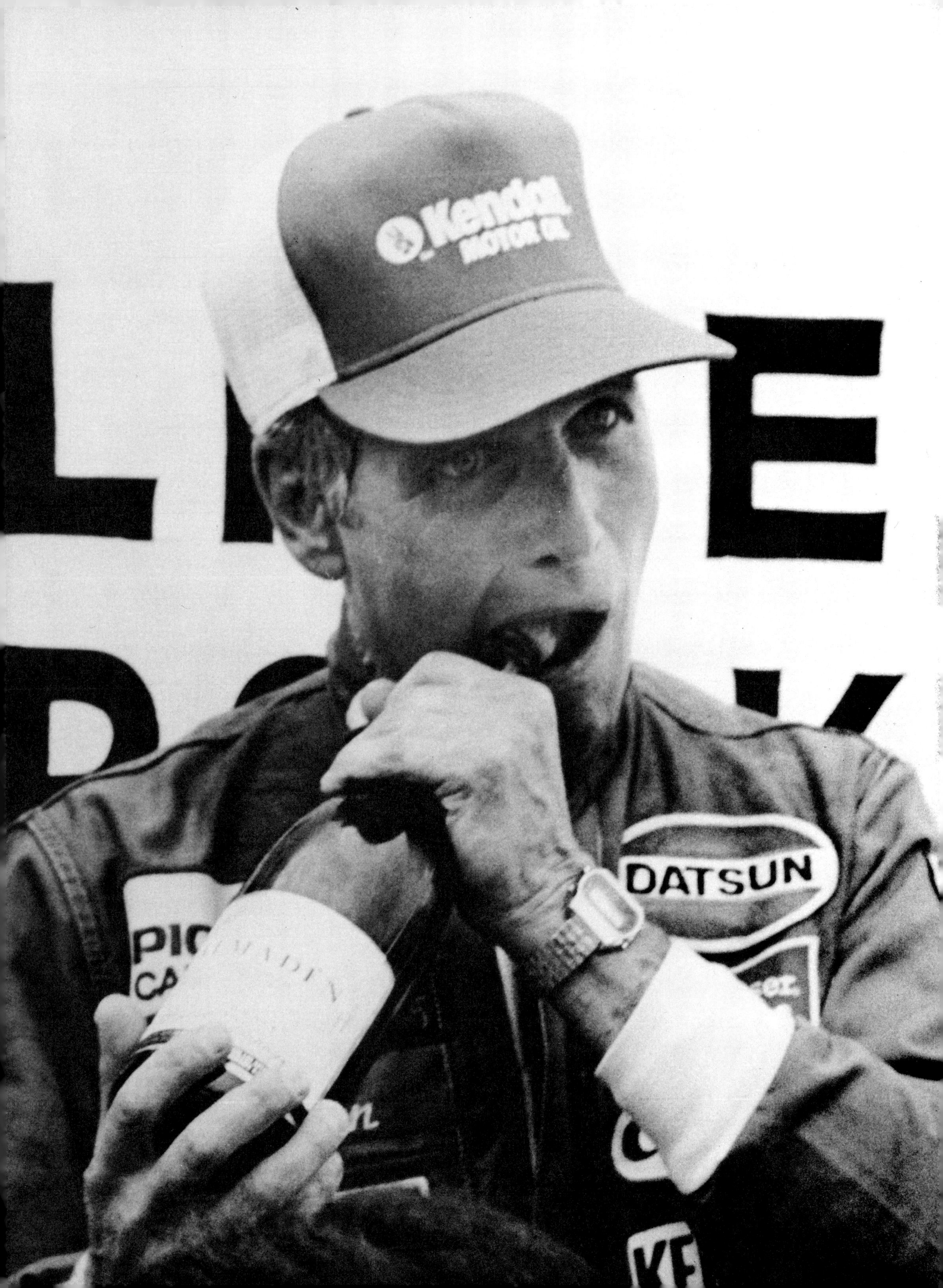
Kendall
MOTOR OIL
DATSUN
DATSUN

Right: Paul Newman with Lord Olivier at the première of
A Little Romance

Below: Newman at the première party for A Little Romance *in honour of Laurence Olivier. Joanne played opposite Olivier in the play (1979)*

Theories abound about why some men choose a lifestyle or profession in which, time and time again, they set themselves at risk. Racing driving is most frequently the example cited and usually the impulse is explained as an unconscious suicidal urge, a death wish disguised by action, skill and drama.

Newman scoffs at this interpretation of his motives. Racing represents something quite different for him. It is the one area of his life where he is not judged by the blueness of his eyes, his popularity or his fame. 'I enjoy racing in any form,' he says, 'because the guy next to me couldn't care less what my name is. He just wants to beat me. At the start of my racing career I had to prove myself. A lot of people think that actors are a little strange, unmasculine . . . I had to beat the actor's image.'

The fact remains that motor racing is the most dangerous of sports. Every race contains risk and despite his protestations – he may genuinely feel that he does not flirt with danger – Newman has more than once experienced some heartstopping moments in his career, coming so close to catastrophe that, but for his luck, he should have died. In 1977, driving a Datsun 510, he competed at Garrettsville, Ohio. During the race a competitor's car went out of control, then shot into the air, before finally slamming down onto the roof of Newman's car. The Datsun collapsed under the impact, encasing its driver inside the wreckage. Miraculously, no one was hurt. On another occasion, the brakes on his Ferrari failed at 130 m.p.h., causing the car to hurtle down an escape road, where it crashed into a building, slicing itself apart. Once again, Newman escaped with only a few bruises. More recently, in 1980, luck stood him in good stead yet again when he emerged unscathed from a 100 m.p.h. pile-up at Lime Rock after his brakes locked.

These incidents did nothing to diminish his enthusiasm and he appeared undaunted by such close shaves. Either the theorists are correct – subconsciously he has a need to set himself at risk – or else Newman must be completely devoid of fear.

In 1979, he faced his toughest challenge – the twenty-four hours at Le Mans, a gruelling race which has claimed many lives during the course of its forty-seven seasons. Newman's team of three drove a 935 Twin Turbo Porsche, reaching speeds of up to 220 m.p.h. He was by far the oldest driver there.

The race also turned out to be the most impressive of his driving achievements. With fifty-five starters, only twenty-two completed the course and Newman's team finished in second place. He had watched his co-driver, Rolf Stommelen, during the last two-and-a-half hours of the race, the tension almost unbearable, for the Porsche was already in second position. At one point the leading car broke down and was repaired on the track as Newman's Porsche passed it and passed again. And then, at a pit stop, eighteen crucial minutes were lost when a jammed wheelnut could not be removed. In the end, engine smoking, it limped across the line. But to come second in the classic event was regarded as a spectacular achievement.

By now Newman's love of racing had been widely publicized and was the one topic on which he was prepared to talk at length. He waxes lyrical on his feeling for the sport: 'I love racing. I wish I could devote every minute of my time to it . . . Racing is the best way I know to get away from the rubbish that goes with being a so-called "Hollywood star". . . I get stoned on cars. For me, they bring out a high. I love the racing game and the people . . . To be behind the wheel of a car doing over 100 m.p.h. is one of the most exhilarating things I know of . . . Racing is a way of being a happy child again.'

How did Miss Woodward adapt to her husband's addiction? She did not share his love for it. 'She thinks competitive driving is the silliest thing in the world,' Newman told Dick Wells of *Motor Trend*, 'it's also very scary for her.' But Joanne accepted this, to her incomprehensible, passion with grace. The Newmans claim that their different interests enhance their relationship. He gravitates towards 'mens' pursuits – cars, sport, beer drinking – while Miss Woodward tends towards the arts – ballet, opera, museums and galleries. 'For a couple who have nothing in common,' she says, 'I guess we're not doing too badly!' Newman adds. 'We are two individuals – and what's wrong with that? Husbands and wives should have separate interests and cultivate different sets of friends. You can't always be breathing down each others necks.' So accepting it as inevitable, Miss Woodward observed, 'I don't go to all his races but then I don't expect him to go to my ballet all the time.'

Newman now feels he is getting a bit long in the tooth for competitive racing, but as yet he has not resigned. He loves cars and will tinker with them for hours in the workshop he has built close to his home, and he can still be found at major events. In 1981 he took part in the Las Vegas Grand Prix, having persuaded the owners of the most famous hotel in town, Caesar's Palace, to build and sponsor this latest Grand Prix circuit. A vast car park was demolished and in its place a million-dollar racing track created.

Newman made a brief appearance at the opening night, a lavish affair at which Tom Jones provided the entertainment. Lovelorn hysterical women, as ever, formed the mass of the well-endowed singer's audience but, on this occasion they turned on Newman and, screaming excitedly, went for him bodily. The mob grew so frantic that Jones had to pull the actor up onto the stage and out of their reach to prevent his being torn to pieces.

He was fifty-seven years old, but clearly he had lost none of his allure.

Actor, director, producer, political activist, the racing driver celebrates with a beer (1982)

12
THE ACCEPTABLE FACE OF SUCCESS

By 1980 Paul Newman had come through the period of his ordeal.

The previous decade had contained more changes, both good and bad, than in the whole of his earlier life. At the start of the 1970s he had achieved superstardom and become the most highly paid actor in the world. A few years later this was followed by professional failure, the death of his son, depression and a mid-life crisis. At the close of the era he emerged emotionally in one piece again with a triumphant series of successes in a totally new field. In a few short years he had experienced a wide span of human experience.

Newman was fortunate in that since youth he had employed his knowledge and awareness of life well; he had sought to understand his confusions as they appeared, rather than allow them to fester unexpressed. This healthy attitude stood him in good stead throughout the tribulations of that decade.

By middle age Newman had achieved that most enviable and hard won condition – maturity, in the full sense of the word. Blessed with a well-balanced disposition, over the years his approach to life was thoughtful and realistic. This stability of character had enabled him to survive intact in Hollywood, retaining his individuality, yet taking the best of what that city can provide. In return, he gave to the industry and to the world a half-dozen films which endure as classics.

'Somebody up there likes me': the tag endures along with the widely shared assumption that Newman has always had it easy whereas, in fact, this myth results from the natural elegance of his style and a horror of demonstrating obvious effort. He has had to face challenge in order to prevail.

As a young actor in 1954 he gained his first film contract because of the colour of his eyes and a passing resemblance to Marlon Brando, and was then cast in a début so appalling it threatened to destroy his career before it had begun. He retrieved the fiasco by achieving a Broadway hit but, right from the start, he was at war with Hollywood. His early battles were waged against the publicity departments and the glossy stereotype they tried to make of him, later developing into conflicts with the studio bosses and their heavy-handed misuse of his talents. His was an unpopular stance, dangerous for a newcomer; only with uncompromising determination and courage did Newman succeed in building his career upon terms which were his own.

Throughout his working life he has taken many chances, always recovering from his failures. He assumed responsibility for his mistakes and errors of judgement, his failures only made him more determined. Never satisfied for long by his achievements, he is strongwilled and a perfectionist in his own work and in what he expects from others. He communicates his passion for excellence. As an employer he is demanding and generous; but his successes are shared by all who are in his team.

Following his greatest triumph in the mid-1970s he fell prey to ennui and disenchantment, renewing his edge only through motor racing. It is with commendable honesty that Newman now speaks of that lapse: 'One thought I've had in my old age is that it's easy for an actor to be corrupted. I always knew it happened to others but I never knew until now that it could happen to me. It's not the money, it's the fact that you start thinking of yourself as a movie star rather than an actor.'

Paul Newman, still a fine figure of a man at fifty-seven

Indeed, for a long time now, he had not needed to make films for money. By his fifties he was a millionaire. For all the flops and decline in popularity that came with them, Newman had never suffered financially. He had been paid handsomely for even the worst of his films. The precedent for big fees had been set by *The Sting*; his next film, *The Towering Inferno*, earning him $2 million and his price remained established, rising with every picture which followed.

Newman had displayed a disgust for his occupation on previous occasions, but invariably he recovered from his distaste when enthusiasm for a specific subject fired him. However, during his worst period of doubt, in his fifties, he considered retiring from films. Why did he not go through with it? 'I have so many friends in the industry,' says Newman, 'that whenever someone asks a favour I have to listen. And on the way up I was helped by innumerable people . . . besides that, Joanne won't leave me alone unless I get out there and do something.' These were largely excuses. Nobody, in the end, can make someone do what they do not want to do. Miss Woodward knew better – acting was in Newman's blood. Eventually even this latest conflict resolved itself. The need to perform, to express himself in the way he knew best, returned. By the end of 1980 Newman was once more taking an interest in scripts: the fire had rekindled.

Now his decision and his choice were crucial. Whatever he appeared in next would be the toughest test of his career; it would make or finish him. 'Newman's luck', those opportunities which, like magic, appeared always at the eleventh hour, were a thing of the past. But without one more kiss from fortune, a less than spectacular return to the screen would condemn him to gradual obscurity. While critical acclaim for a performance was essential, so also was a renewal of his popularity. It was vital that he regained the audiences who had flocked to see him in the early 1970s. Whether he liked it or not, despite his talent, Newman's career successes derived from his unique brand of appeal, his 'star quality'. He was of that exclusive breed – albeit fading – the Big Star. Few remained of these, in the traditional sense of the word, and Newman's comeback depended on living up to the expectation and the myth. He had faced a similar challenge before, but this time the stakes were higher.

In 1981 he found the script that fitted these exacting requirements. The completed film itself would cause controversy, but from Newman's personal point of view it was the perfect vehicle in which to correct the most serious problem of his career.

Fort Apache – The Bronx was a highly emotive, racy, police drama. All human life was there, and the film was possessed of that elusive element – popular appeal. Newman starred as Murphy, a New York cop. Anti-authoritarian, involved, individual, he was a classic Newman character ten years on. Murphy is concerned about the social ills he sees around him, and there is no human drama in which he does not put himself into the heart – at one point delivering a baby in the street.

A Hollywood Phenomenon. The long and happy marriage

Right: Newman, typically surrounded by adoring females, supporting MeGovern in 1972

Below: A man of many parts, Newman campaigns for McGovern at Madison Square Gardens, 1972

The movie received some harsh and detailed criticism – but in every review one aspect was unequivocally praised. Paul Newman's performance was a triumph – he carried the movie. Because Murphy is so attractive, because it is impossible not to like him, the film, in spite of its appalling flaws, comes off superbly. In 1982 *New Society* summed up this victory over both a bad script and the questionable moral of its message: 'Newman is able to deliver even the clumsiest lines with more than a semblance of conviction . . . his performance is an object lesson on how to hold a movie together with a combination of irresistible charm and perfect technique.'

The controversy the film caused stemmed from two factions. First, the local inhabitants of the community in which the picture was located protested strongly at the way their neighbourhood had been misinterpreted. Ordinary men and women from the Bronx felt the movie grossly exaggerated the crime and violence of the area. They were insulted by the poor and useless image of their lives as portrayed on the screen. Others found the film repugnant, and this second major criticism was directed towards its producers – for their insensitivity in choosing an emotive script calculated to offend and provoke the community it portrayed. Both producer David Susskind and director Don Petrie, like their star, were supposedly committed 'liberals'. How then, many asked, could they have created a film that degraded the powerless by its banal 'macho' approach, one more suited to the old attitudes expressed in the late John Wayne movies? In the social climate of the 1980s, *Fort Apache*'s basic premise, that all it takes to deal with the world's ills is one tough, sexy cop with a conscience, was seen to be patronizing and dishonest.

However the picture was received by the public everywhere with enthusiasm. In an age when self-assertion and aggression are fashionable, this tough guy theme was welcomed. The film did very well commercially and, most importantly, restored Newman's rating at the box office. For all that was wrong with the film, it was right for him.

As a star, he was back on top. Any doubts about his motives in appearing in that picture were forgiven overnight when his next was released.

Absence of Malice, directed by Sidney Pollack, was not only a greater commercial success than *Fort Apache – The Bronx*, it was widely acclaimed as a thoughtful and courageous film. Its theme is the power without responsibility of the Press, a subject of particular interest to Newman who, a few years before, had suffered impotently from its attack. In the film he plays the son of a dead gangster, who is running a legitimate business. His link by birth to the mobsters, who still control the town, make him a suspect when a local labour leader disappears, assumed dead, at the hands of the mob. His name is leaked to an over-zealous reporter, played by Sally Field, who exposes the story. Unable to prove malice, his only defence, the wronged man loses his friends and eventually his business. The truth finally is aired only when it is too late; the journalist is fired from her job but by then Newman is quitting town, his life irreparably damaged.

Crisply made, provocative enough to raise important questions, *Absence of Malice* was the best film Newman had

Back on top in Absence of Malice, *1981*

ndard
Final
Edition
allagher Not Involved
n Diaz Case" --Quinn
Senator's Upset Loss
to be Felt in Education

appeared in for years. He was tremendous in his role, as good as he had ever been. In spite of its serious, political theme, audiences flocked to see the movie.

Newman had done it again. Like the true professional he is, once more he had picked himself up and delivered a superlative performance and in 1982 he received yet another Oscar nomination.

Nothing is more fragile than box office popularity, yet Newman has won it, lost it, and regained it not once but many times. It is a remarkable feat.

Aged fifty-nine, looking forty-five, he is untroubled by the passing of the years. He has elected to fill the parts he now fills, 'I can't do young roles forever', he says 'nor play the same old studs or playboys.' Later in 1982 he began filming in a promising venture entitled *The Verdict* in which he plays a lawyer, starring with Charlotte Rampling and James Mason.

Aside from acting and cars, Newman has lately been concentrating on the problems of drink and drug abuse. After his son died, the Newmans created the Scott Newman Foundation in his memory. The aim of the Foundation is to guide and inform young people on drug abuse, to reach them before they become victims, and to help give their lives purpose since Scott's life had held tragically little meaning for him. In 1981, Newman quietly went to work on another kind of film, *Say No*, a project aimed at helping youngsters resist the ever-present temptations of drink and drugs. His personal experience makes him a compelling lobbyist, and his whole family is involved with the Foundation's work. Newman says, 'Youth is a difficult period of life. We all tend, when we're older, to say children and teenagers are living out the best times of their lives, but those are actually the scariest, the most insecure and confusing. It's not until one is adult that one's head is in the right place, if it's ever going to be. I've been, in general, enjoying my years since thirty and since forty more than those that went before.'

His marriage to Joanne Woodward endures; another of the major successes of his life. Their secret, apart from love, has always lain in their respect for and tolerance of each other, not only during the good times but also through the bad. 'I don't think you can get impatient with each other,' says Newman. 'We are all flawed, you know, and you've got to love each other so that those flaws aren't taken out of context.'

Fourteen years ago, in an interview with Richard Warren Lewis, Newman spoke of how he would like to be remembered when he died. Today, still in perfect health, he has already triumphantly achieved all the goals to which he aspired.

'I would like to leave the memory of a man who has tried to be of his time, tried to help people to communicate with each other, tried to bring out something decent in his own life. The memory of someone who has known how to grow without too much celebrating his own victories, the memory of someone who has not been completely satisfied with himself. The memory of someone who has not been wiped out by set-backs. You have to keep trying. That's the most important thing.'

EPILOGUE

On the eve of the Academy Awards in April 1983, for the sixth time in his twenty-nine-year career, Paul Newman was nominated for an Oscar for his portrayal of a drunken lawyer in *The Verdict*.

The film tells the story of a run-down attorney who finds himself with one last chance to redeem his self-respect. The character offered Newman one of his meatiest roles to date. His performance in the picture, his forty-eighth, was considered by many to be the triumph of his career. As always, Newman researched his part and was well equipped to play the alcoholic. As a young man he had saved himself from that hell only just in time.

The Verdict received glowing critical acclaim. For Newman personally it was a spectacular success, re-establishing beyond doubt a reputation that had flagged, largely as a result of appearances in a series of abysmal projects in the late 70s. But the genius which had held audiences spellbound in such classics as *The Hustler* and *Hud* had re-emerged. A typical review proclaimed: '. . . his performance is brilliant. . . . Newman's a shoo-in for this year's Oscar as Best Actor.'

Paul Newman did not win the Oscar on that April evening. He is a philosophical man, but, sixth time round, it *would* have been good finally to hold that coveted award.

'I have mixed feelings about the Academy Awards,' says Newman. 'How can anyone, even the most astute members . . . decide which is better, apples or oranges? . . . Different actors, in greatly different roles, competing . . . who can say who is best? That's why I am absolutely non-competitive about acting. . . .' Perhaps that's why the actor gets so much satisfaction from racing cars. In this, almost a second career, he is *very* competitive. Heading for sixty, Newman is still a demon on the tracks. 'If you're the first one across the finish line,' he says, 'there's no room for argument. You have positively *won*.'

With acting, the rules are more oblique. Unexpected factors can affect the final reaction to a film—*The Verdict* is an example. There are always minorities who will cavil where the majority applaud and it transpired that a faction of the legal profession objected that the film was 'controversial.' The theme of the lone misfit pitched against a powerful system—which they represented—and *winning*, was not popular.

Newman, since it was he who played the recalcitrant, unorthodox lawyer, became associated with this debate. It is not possible to say if it affected his chances at the Academy Awards. It is well known, however, that Hollywood is notorious for its convention, and the whole affair caused damaging publicity, staining the reputation of a fine picture that boasts one of the most superb performances of that year.

On January 29th, 1983, Paul Newman celebrated twenty-five years of marriage to actress Joanne Woodward.

This is a remarkable feat in a world where brief unions are the norm. How did the Newmans survive a Hollywood marriage? In such marriages the couple invariably have a shared humour, and it is usual to find that one has made more compromises than the other. Humour has aided the Newmans through the hard times, and Joanne has made the most compromises. Her talent, as seen with and without her husband, is highly respected, but she has always put home and family first.

Newman says of his wife, 'She's a mercurial lady. I never know what I'm going to wake up with. . . . Our marriage involves two people with very different approaches and attitudes. . . . There's affection and respect. . . .We've managed to come through together.'

And Joanne? 'I can't conceive of life without Paul,' she says. 'He makes me feel beautiful . . .'

What of Newman today? After twenty years the couple have left the rambling Westport house and moved to a smaller home by the Aspetuck river. The old house won't be sold but kept for the girls. None of the five daughters has followed in her father's footsteps, though two have shown they have the talent.

Meanwhile, the actor thrives. An incredibly youthful fifty-nine, Newman takes good care of himself. He works hard at living a healthy life. Most mornings he'll run three miles and is an adept skiier, tennis player and swimmer.

It's hard to find a good script these days. Dutifully, he looks at between 400 and 500 a year. But Newman always manages to surprise his admirers. He once swore never to act again in a movie he was directing. Now, not only is he starring in and directing his next venture, he co-scripted as well. The working title is *Harry's Boy* or *Harry and Son*. It is not based on Newman's relationship with his own son, Scott, who died tragically at twenty-eight though. Newman has hinted that one day he would like to make a film about his tormented first-born's life. Profits from *Harry's Boy* will be donated to the Scott Newman Foundation, set up to discourage drug abuse and in memory of Scott.

Newman's annual income exceeds $2 million. He still cares deeply about certain issues and is generous with his anonymous contributions to these causes. Always an astute businessman, recently he's entered a completely new field—patenting his very own Newman's Salad Dressing with great success.

Another future ambition includes working once more with Robert Redford and director George Roy Hill. 'George directed us in *Butch Cassidy* and *The Sting*,' says Newman, 'and ever since then the three of us have been looking for another picture to do together.'

Newman is one of the last of the Hollywood Greats. To outsiders he can seem enigmatic, even cold. The impression is false. His close friend, the otherwise cynical Gore Vidal, says, 'Paul is one of the few people I know who has a good character.'

SOURCES

Paul Newman, Charles Hamblett (W. H. Allen, London 1975).

Paul Newman Superstar, Lionel Godfrey (Hale, London 1978).

The Films of Paul Newman, Laurence J. Quirk (Citadel Press, New York, paperback 1973).

Article by Richard Goldstein, *Voice*, 14 April 1980.

Article by Andrew Tudor, *New Society*, 11 February 1982.

'The Redoubtable Mr Newman' by Grover Lewis, *Rolling Stone*, July 1973.

Article by Michael Billington, *The Times*, 8 February 1982.

'Newman's Complaint' by Roger Ebert, *Esquire*, September 1969.

Interview by M. G. Haddad *Photoplay*, June 1979.

'Class Dues', *Newsweek*, December 1978.

'Hollywood's Blue-eyed Boy' by Jane Wilson, *Sunday Times* 1969.

Interview by Richard Warren Lewis, *Playboy*, June 1968.

FILMOGRAPHY

1955	The Silver Chalice	*Warner Brothers*
1956	The Rack	*M.G.M.*
1957	Somebody Up There Likes Me	*M.G.M.*
1957	The Helen Morgan Story	*Warner Brothers*
1957	Until They Sail	*M.G.M.*
1958	The Long Hot Summer	*20th Century Fox*
1958	The Left-Handed Gun	*Warner Brothers*
1958	Cat on a Hot Tin Roof	*M.G.M.*
1959	Rally Round the Flag, Boys!	*20th Century Fox*
1959	The Young Philadelphians	*Warner Brothers*
1960	From the Terrace	*20th Century Fox*
1960	Exodus	*United Artists*
1961	The Hustler	*20th Century Fox*
1961	Paris Blues	*United Artists*
1962	Sweet Bird of Youth	*M.G.M.*
1962	Hemingway's Adventures of a Young Man	*20th Century Fox*
1963	Hud	*Paramount*
1963	A New Kind of Love	*Paramount*
1963	The Prize	*M.G.M.*
1964	The Outrage	*M.G.M.*
1964	What a Way to Go	*20th Century Fox*
1966	Lady L	*M.G.M.*
1967	The Moving Target	*Warner Brothers*
1967	Torn Curtain	*Universal*
1967	Hombre	*20th Century Fox*
1967	Cool Hand Luke	*Warner Brothers*
1968	Rachel, Rachel (director only)	*Warner Brothers*
1968	The Secret War of Harry Frigg	*Universal*
1968	Winning	*Universal*
1968	Butch Cassidy and the Sundance Kid	*20th Century Fox*
1969	W.U.S.A.	*Paramount*
1970	Sometimes a Great Notion (star and director)	*Universal*
1971	Pocket Money	*National General*
1971	The Life and Times of Judge Roy Bean	*National General*
1972	The Effect of Gamma Rays on the Man-in-the-Moon Marigolds (director only)	*Universal*
1973	The Mackintosh Man	*Warner Brothers*
1973	The Sting	*Universal*
1974	The Towering Inferno	*20th Century Fox*
1974	The Drowning Pool	*Warner Brothers*
1976	Buffalo Bill and the Indians	*E.M.I.*
1976	Silent Movie	*20th Century Fox*
1977	Slap Shot	*Universal*
1979	Quintet	*Warner Brothers*
1980	When Time Ran Out	*Warner Brothers*
1981	Fort Apache – The Bronx	*20th Century Fox*
1982	Absence of Malice	*Columbia*
1983	The Verdict	*20th Century Fox*

PHOTO ACKNOWLEDGEMENTS

The author and publishers are grateful to those listed below for supplying and/or giving permission to reproduce the following illustrations:

page 1; Ron Galella; 2, Aquarius/Jalem Productions; 4–5, Aquarius/Paramount-Salem-Dover Productions; 6, Ron Galella; 8, Aquarius/Paramount-Salem-Dover Productions; 11, 13, Aquarius; 15, Peter C. Borsari; 16, Aquarius; 19, 21, 22, Ron Galella; 24–5, 26, Aquarius/M.G.M.; 28, Ron Galella; 30, Associated Press; 31, Ron Galella; 32, 33, Aquarius; 34, Ron Galella; 35, Fotos International, photo by Frank Edwards; 36, Aquarius; 37, Aquarius/Warner Brothers; 38, Fotos International, photo by Frank Edwards; 39, Peter C. Borsari; 41, Aquarius; 42, United Press International; 44–5, Aquarius; 46, Ron Galella; 48, 50, Aquarius/M.G.M.; 51, Aquarius/ 20th Century Fox; 52, Aquarius; 55, Aquarius/20th Century Fox; 56, Aquarius/Paramount-Salem-Dover Productions; 59, 60–1, Aquarius/20th Century Fox; 63, Syndication International; 64–5 (3), Aquarius/M.G.M.; 66, United Press International; 68, Aquarius/Jalem Productions; 70–1, Rank Films; 72, 75, 76, Ron Galella; 79, Associated Press; 80, Ron Galella; 82–3, Syndication International; 84, 87, Ron Galella; 88–9, 20th Century Fox; 90–1, Syndication International, photo by Peter Stone; 93, Ron Galella; 95, Syndication International/ Keystone Press; 96, Associated Press; 97, Fox Photos; 98, Betty Burke Galella; 101, Syndication International; 102 (top), Ron Galella; 102 (bottom), Camera Press/Twenty Pimlico Ltd; 103, Transworld Feature Syndicate, photo by David Sutton; 104, 105, 107, 108, Ron Galella; 109, *National Enquirer*; 110, Ron Galella; 113, Syndication International; 114, Ron Galella; 117, Universal Pictures; 118, Univesal Press; 119 (2), 120, Ron Galella; 122, Syndication International; 123, Peter C. Borsari; 124–5, 126, Ron Galella; 127, Betty Burke Galella; 128, Ron Galella; 129, Peter C. Borsari; 131, Ron Galella; 132, Betty Burke Galella; 135, 136, 137, Ron Galella; 139, Universal Press.

INDEX

Page numbers in italics refer to illustrations.